RETURN TO REASON

RETURN TO REASON
An Introduction to Objectivism

PAUL LEPANTO

Exposition Press   *New York*

EXPOSITION PRESS INC.

50 Jericho Turnpike   Jericho, New York 11753

FIRST EDITION

© 1971 by Paul Lepanto. *All rights reserved, including the right of reproduction in whole or in part in any form except for short quotations in critical essays and reviews.* Manufactured in the United States of America.

0-682-47204-2

To my wife

MARTHA

who has earned the rarest distinction of all for she is a truly human being

Contents

Preface ... 9

PART ONE

1. Existence ... 13
2. Life ... 17

PART TWO

3. Our Senses ... 21
4. Concepts ... 29
5. Logic ... 33
6. Volitional Consciousness ... 38
7. Values ... 42
8. Reason, Purpose, Self-Esteem ... 45
9. Morality ... 49
10. Duality of Awareness ... 53
11. Art ... 56
12. The Subconscious ... 59
13. Emotions ... 63
14. Emotional Perplexities ... 66
15. Repression ... 71
16. Self-Esteem ... 74
17. A Summary and a Preview ... 78

PART THREE

18. Knowledge and Progress ... 81
19. Production and Trade ... 84
20. Visibility ... 90
21. Sexuality ... 95

22	*The Nature of Freedom*	100
23	*Freedom in Society*	103
24	*Rights: I*	107
25	*Rights: II*	113
26	*The Role of Government*	119
27	*Censorship*	124
28	*Prohibitionism*	128
29	*Conscription*	132
30	*Taxation*	135
31	*Evaluating Government Practices*	139
32	*Capitalism*	144
33	*Social Metaphysics and Spiritual Appeasement*	148
34	*A Rational Way of Life*	153

Preface

Before getting underway, I'd like to make two important points:

1. For several years, I have been a student of the only rational school of contemporary philosophy: objectivism. This book is a product of those years of study. I frankly and gratefully acknowledge my intellectual indebtedness to Ayn Rand and Nathaniel Branden, and to their associates who have contributed to the growth of objectivism. This I want to say, so as not to be guilty of intellectual plagiarism.

2. However, this book is solely my own work, based upon my understanding of rational philosophy. I am *not* a spokesman for Miss Rand, nor for anyone else—except myself. I am not personally acquainted with Miss Rand or her associates, past or present; I know them only through their works. I do not know what evaluation Miss Rand will make of this book, if she chooses to make any at all. This I want to say, so as not to be guilty of intellectual fraud.

There are already several sources of information available to persons wishing to learn about objectivism. Of course, Miss Rand's novels, especially *Atlas Shrugged,* are of crucial importance and value. As it happens, though, many readers find that they can learn philosophy most effectively from a straightforward philosophical treatment rather than from works of fiction, however superb such works may be. Such a treatment was offered by Nathaniel Branden Institute, but that organization has recently closed its doors.

Sources like the *Objectivist* (formerly the *Objectivist Newsletter*), the official journal of objectivism, do deal with philosophical issues directly but on what might be called intermediate or advanced levels. This publication is a philosophical journal and therefore is not intended to serve as a "course" in objectivism. Just as a student beginning a study of physics may find journals of physics a bit over his head until he has studied the basics, a student of objectivism may experience a need for a basic nonfictional treatment of the philosophy so that he can better profit from the *Objectivist* and from books like *The Virtue of Selfishness, Capitalism: The Unknown Ideal,* and *The Romantic Manifesto.*

This book has been written to meet that need.

References are made to sources which the reader may wish to consult. Most are to the *Objectivist* (or the *Objectivist Newsletter,* as it was known from 1962 through 1965), and appear as numbers in parentheses. A typical reference might be: (5/66, 2); this indicates the May, 1966, issue, page 2.

Anyone who is even partially conscious knows that humanity is in big trouble—politically, economically, socially, culturally, intellectually, and morally. Rather than labor the obvious, I offer one brief observation: the solutions to man's problems can be found only after a return to reason.

P. L.

PART ONE

1 Existence

The central idea in rational philosophy is *existence*. This idea is at the heart of all other concepts, and so we begin with some observations about existence.

To begin with, the concept of existence is inescapable. The mind is quite unable to reject it. One could state, of course, "Nothing exists," but it would be absurd to do so. Clearly, the person who makes such a statement must exist; a non-existent person cannot make any statement. It makes no difference how carefully the statement is phrased; the fact remains that you cannot dispute the idea of existence without assuming in the process that something or someone does in fact exist. In other words, any attempt to deny the concept of existence defeats itself.

Because it is inescapable, the concept of existence is described as *axiomatic*, that is, self-evident.

If we try to define existence, we face a formidable problem indeed. A statement like "Existence is being" seems most unsatisfactory; after all, what is "being?" But we need not be embarrassed by the gambit, "If existence is so important, go ahead and define it." The plain fact is that existence is not formally definable.

Here is why: Whenever we define a thing we must classify it; we must place it in some category broader than itself. For instance, we can define a square as an equilateral rectangle, thereby classifying squares into the broader category of rectangles. (The definition also tells us how squares differ from other rectangles—those that are not equilateral.) Now, if we are to define existence, we must be able to place it in some broader category. But the very concept of existence already contains *everything;* and what can be broader than that? In other words, there is no category broader than existence itself. Since we can't classify existence, and since definition requires our classifying the thing to be defined, it follows that existence is not formally definable.

The best we can do by way of defining existence is to use the so-called ostensive definition. In this approach we display something in order to define it. For instance, one might ostensively define "green" by pointing to grass and saying, "By green I mean the color of this." In this manner one can sweep one's arm around and say, "By existence I mean all of this." But as for giving a formal definition of existence, this we cannot do, as explained earlier.

Consider now these two statements:
1. Dinosaurs exist.
2. Dinosaurs do not exist.

Can both statements be simultaneously correct? Evidently not. Just as the mind immediately grasps the concept of existence, so certain laws that pertain to existence are also self-evident. Thus we know that dinosaurs cannot simultaneously exist and yet not exist. In other words, the alternatives of (1) existence and (2) non-existence are *mutually exclusive.*

Suppose, now, it was claimed that neither of the above two statements about dinosaurs is correct, that it is wrong to say that dinosaurs exist and also wrong to say that they do not. We would reject such a claim. In addition to being mutually exclusive, the alternatives of existence and non-existence are also *jointly exhaustive.* In other words, there is no third alternative to (1) existence and (2) non-existence. A thing either is or is not.

So there are two alternatives: existence and non-existence. They are mutually exclusive, and there is no third alternative. Either dinosaurs exist or else they do not; it cannot be both ways, and there is no third possibility. Either a leaf is entirely green or it is not entirely green. It cannot be green all over and yet at the same time have red spots. Nor is there any third alternative to its being (1) all green or (2) not all green.

Either the sun generates heat or it does not generate heat; it must be one way or the other, and cannot be both.

A piece of iron is either (1) entirely solid, or (2) not entirely solid (e.g., liquid, gaseous, half-solid and half-liquid, etc.); it cannot be entirely solid and yet partly liquid at the same time. Nor can a piece of iron be in a state not falling under one of two headings (1) entirely solid, (2) not entirely solid.

Of course, it is possible for a piece of iron to change from solid to some other state, say liquid. But at any one time it must be one or the other. We are certainly not denying that things can and do undergo changes. A leaf can change from green to red, but it cannot be all green and all red simultaneously.

In these examples we have considered entities, that is, objects (dinosaurs, a leaf, the sun, a piece of iron), attributes of entities (color of a leaf, solid or non-solid state of iron), and actions of entities (the sun generating heat). The fact is that anything we choose to consider—entity, attribute, action—must be of a specific kind, having certain definite characteristics and lacking others. That is to say, it must have a definite *identity*. A leaf, the sun, iron—each has specific characteristics, a specific nature. A leaf is a leaf, not a stone. The color green is a specific attribute, different from red. The solid state has properties of its own, quite different from those of the liquid or the gaseous states. Generating heat is one action; writing a symphony is another.

Again we find ourselves inescapably aware of a basic law of existence: whatever exists has a specific nature or identity that makes it uniquely what it is; it is something, not just anything, and not nothing. This is the *Law of Identity*.

As mentioned earlier, we are not denying the fact of change. A leaf can change from green to red. A solid piece of iron can be melted. Eons into the future the sun may burn out and cease to generate heat. In past eons dinosaurs did exist, but they are no longer found on our planet. The laws of existence reviewed above do not contradict all this; in fact, they make the phenomenon of change understandable.

At any one time, in any one set of circumstances, a thing

either is or is not; and if it exists, then it exists as something definite and determined, something having a specific nature. This specific nature determines the attributes it can have, the actions it can perform, and the changes it can undergo. It is because a leaf is what it is that it can turn from green to red under certain conditions. It is the nature of the sun to generate heat and light; the nature of a stone prevents *it* from doing so too. It is the nature of iron to melt at a certain temperature; it is the nature of water to boil at a certain temperature.

We must stress the fact that actions are actions *of entities*. Clearly, there can be no action without some entity to do the acting. There can be no changing of color, no generating of heat, no melting, without some object or entity to perform these actions.

What an entity is determines what it can do, as well as what it will do, in a given context of circumstances. A thing cannot act in contradiction to its nature; to *act* differently, it would have to *be* different. Its action is a partial expression of its identity. This is the *Law of Causality*.

The action of one object may affect another object in some way. For example, the sun warms an ice cube, and the ice cube melts. The sun, through its action, affects the ice cube, causing it to melt. We can say that this second action, the melting, is a reaction to the sun's action of warming. An action is often a reaction to some previous action—often, but not always.

A living entity, for example, can initiate many of its own actions. A dog that is lying down can get up and walk; a man can initiate a process of thought to solve a complex problem. The distinction between the living and the non-living is just this: living entities can initiate actions while lifeless ones cannot.

We'll be examining the nature of life in a later chapter. The point being stressed here is that not every action is a reaction to some previous action. There is an unfortunate tendency to lose sight of this fact.

The cause of an action is an entity, not some prior action. The Law of Causality tells us that an action *always* proceeds from an entity according to the nature of that entity; it may or may not be a reaction to some previous action that affected the entity.

2 Life

Any action must be the action of some entity. It may be a reaction to some prior action affecting the entity, or it may be originated by the entity itself.

Nathaniel Branden contrasts these two situations in this way (3/66, 10): A stone cannot of its own accord start moving. It can move only as a result of forces acting on it, as when it rolls down a hill in reaction to the force of gravity. On the other hand, a dog can initiate his own motion. A dog that is lying down can of his own accord start to walk or run.

The dog may act in response to something in his environment, such as a dish of food set on the floor. It is sometimes argued that the dog's action of getting up and going over to the food is merely a physical reaction to the placing of the food on the floor. But careful consideration will show that this is not correct. After all, the dish of food does not physically pull the dog to it, as a magnet pulls a nail. The actual physical motion originates in the dog himself. The action of walking is *self-generated;* it is not the same as being pulled to the dish.

This simple case, a dog's rousing himself and eating, points up the three main characteristics of any living organism: (1) Its life is conditional; there is always the danger of death. (2) It is capable of self-generated action. (3) Such action can, and under appropriate conditions will, sustain its life. In the previous example of the dog: (1) The dog will perish without food. (2) The dog is capable of initiating actions, such as walking to his dish and eating from it. (3) These actions help to sustain his life.

The capacity for such action makes living organisms very special. Non-living things can only react passively to forces acting on them. A stone falls because of the gravitational action of the earth on it. The sun radiates energy because of the nuclear activity that is occuring within it. Neither can initiate any action to sustain itself. Neither has the capacities mentioned by Branden (1/66, 8) as typical of life: growth, maturation, self-healing, self-generated actions in relation to environment. Such goal-directed behavior belongs only to living things.

Living things exist on three levels: plants, animals, and man. It will prove useful to examine each level briefly to see what the levels have in common and how they differ.

Plants are the simplest form of life. For a plant to survive, its environment must provide it with certain things (sunlight, water, various chemicals, etc.). If the environment provides these things, the plant will function automatically and survive by taking nourishment, repairing itself, and so on. In an unsuitable environment the plant will perish.

To sum up: A plant is "programmed" by its nature to function automatically to further its own life; whether or not it succeeds depends upon whether or not its environment provides for its needs.

An animal is a more advanced organism. Like a plant it must be in a favorable environment in order to grow and live. But an animal has powers that a plant lacks. An animal can move around (power of locomotion) and has senses that make him conscious (aware) of his environment. He often uses his power of locomotion to further his life, as when hunting for food or fleeing from an enemy. Furthermore, his senses provide his consciousness with information which can help him to survive, for example, the fact that a dish of food has been set on the floor for him.

An animal has a built-in incentive system to reward life-serving action and to penalize life-harming action: his pleasure-pain mechanism. Something that is beneficial to the life of the animal, like eating, is generally pleasurable. An action that harms the animal, like going too close to a fire, is painful. The sensations of pleasure and pain are of inestimable help to him in his fight for survival.

To sum up: An animal has wider powers than a plant, but like a plant, is programmed by nature to function automatically

Life

for his own survival. Whether he lives or dies depends upon the suitability of his environment.

We can see at once that man has certain things in common with lower forms of life. Man needs a suitable environment, one able to provide oxygen, water, food, etc. Like animals, man is conscious, able to move about, and equipped with a pleasure-pain system. Things that make man different from lower forms of life include his power to think rationally and his free will. More will be said about man's special abilities later, but first we have a hypothetical experiment to consider.

Suppose that a dog were drugged so as to suspend his consciousness and locomotion. Could he survive? Yes, if we saw to it that his vital needs were attended to. But he would be surviving in a manner appropriate to a lower level of life. We would say, quite aptly, that he had been reduced to a vegetable, because he would be functioning like a plant instead of an animal. And we would ponder the question whether a dog permanently in such a state is not virtually dead in view of his functioning not like a dog but rather like a lower form of life.

Note further that while such a dog could continue to live under laboratory conditions, he would quickly perish if left alone in the wilderness. Unable to respond consciously to his surroundings or to hunt for food, he would die.

While a plant can survive without the powers of consciousness and locomotion, because its nature permits it to do so, an animal cannot survive that way. *Its* nature is to function differently.

In other words, how an organism survives depends upon what it is. This conclusion is a special case of the Law of Causality.

The experiment just considered implies the following generalization: An organism has, according to its nature, a specific manner of survival appropriate to it. It cannot survive on any lower level except under artificial conditions, and even if it does it might as well be dead.

Man, too, has a definite nature from which follows his proper method of survival. Man has the power to think, and this power is the key to his manner of living. In upcoming chapters we'll examine in detail just what this means. For now, bear in mind that the accomplishments of man—from the growing of food to the lauching of spacecraft—have come from his thinking mind. He may use his muscles to implement his mind's decisions, but it is his mind that forwards his life and generates his progress.

Man must live by his mind. Let anyone who doubts this ask whether man could survive in any lesser manner.

Suppose that as the result of some dreadful disease, a man's consciousness were reduced to the level of a dog's. Such a man could survive only in a situation in which all his needs were provided for, as in a hospital.

How well would he do in the wilderness? A man is not very strong physically, nor very swift. He doesn't even have a dog's acute sense of smell. With luck he might find some plants whose parts he could stuff into his mouth in order to fend off starvation for a while. But even if he did survive for a week or two, it would be a living death: a man's functioning on a sub-human level of life.

Man, like other organisms, has by nature a proper manner of survival. A man cannot survive in any other manner without virtually or literally dying. A dog can survive without rational thought; a man cannot.

Bear in mind that man has the power of choice as well as the ability to think. Unlike plants and animals, which function in their own interest automatically, a man must perform his highest function, thought, by choice. It is possbile (though very bad) for him to evade the task of thinking. This fact will prove crucial in our consideration of man and his life.

It would be rare for a person to descend to the level of an animal as in the example above. But there are other ways in which a human being can default on his responsibility to live as his nature indicates he should. We are about to turn our attention to the nature of man, to his proper manner of survival, and to the costly mistakes that some people make by trying to escape their human nature.

PART TWO

Part Two deals with man as an individual.

So much is made nowadays of the social aspect of human nature that many people feel that little of any real significance can be learned about man unless he is studied as a social being.

But man is primarily an individual being.

The reader may be surprised to discover how very much of what is important about man's life can be learned prior to any consideration of man as a social being.

(The social side of human existence will be covered in Part Three.)

3 Our Senses

Consciousness, like existence, is an axiomatic concept. Each of us experiences consciousness (awareness) of himself and his surroundings, and we are quite unable to evade this fact. If someone were to demand that you prove you are conscious, he would be committing a crude fallacy. Proof pertains to knowledge and knowledge presupposes the ability to know, which is consciousness. Anyone demanding a proof of consciousness is actually assuming the fact of consciousness by his very act of asking for proof.

Axiomatic ideas are usually related, and the relation between existence and consciousness is this: it is through your consciousness that you gain knowledge of existing reality; existence is the *object* of consciousness. A thing has a definite identity; we *identify* it through our consciousness.

The thing of which a person is most intimately conscious is himself. No one can seriously doubt or deny his own existence. After all, if he didn't exist, how could he perform the action of doubting or denying anything? In order to live, however, a man must also know about things outside himself so that he can act effectively to further his life.

We are going to take a close look at man's consciousness, and the first thing to consider is man's senses.

While man is distinguished by the fact that his mind can function on higher levels than mere sensory perception, the old adage is still true: there is nothing in the intellect that is not first in the senses. If a person were afflicted at birth in such a way that none of his senses functioned, how active could his intellect be? What could he ever know about the universe around him? All the channels of information from the outside world would be closed to him, and his mind would remain forever blank. A man's senses are his window on the universe. Through them he learns things that he can use to further his life.

But how, exactly? Granted that a human being, like any other organism, faces the alternatives of life or death, how do his senses help him to sustain his life?

First of all, man possesses a pleasure-pain system. Generally speaking, actions beneficial to life are pleasurable, while those harmful to life are painful. Pleasure is a reward for beneficial action and an incentive to make further use of such action. Pain is a penalty for harmful action and a deterrent to persisting in such action. It is through the experiences of pleasure and pain that you first face the alternatives of efficacy and inefficacy in sustaining your life. (5/66, 2).

Furthermore, the things you learn through your senses can be retained in your memory for future reference. In this way knowledge grows in your mind. This is a tremendous advantage, since otherwise you would have to relearn every lesson again and again.

While animals also have pleasure-pain mechanisms and memories, man derives an additional benefit from his senses, and it is his alone, not shared by any lower form of life. This benefit is that information gained through his senses can be identified and integrated by his highest faculty: reason. Rational thought is man's highest power and as we have seen, the key to his proper mode of survival. But before examining reason more closely, we must be sure to appreciate the value of our senses, which supply the raw data for reason to work with.

Unfortunately there exists some misunderstanding about the reliability of the senses. It is sometimes said that our senses distort things and deceive us so that the world as we see it is not the world as it is. Let's examine this notion more closely.

Whenever I perceive a thing, my senses produce what we may call sense data relating back to the thing perceived. On the basis of past experience my mind interprets the data and draws a conclusion about the thing being perceived. We may symbolize the process like this:

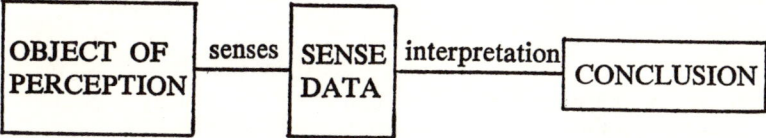

To take a specific example, suppose I look at a cube and recognize it. The process would be:

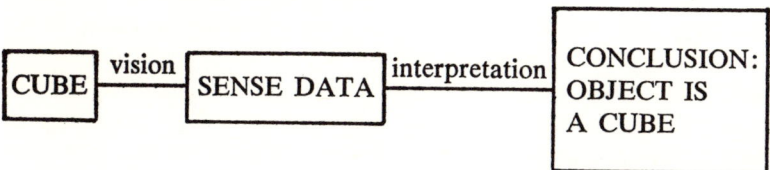

Now, suppose that my conclusion is that the object is not a cube but a pyramid:

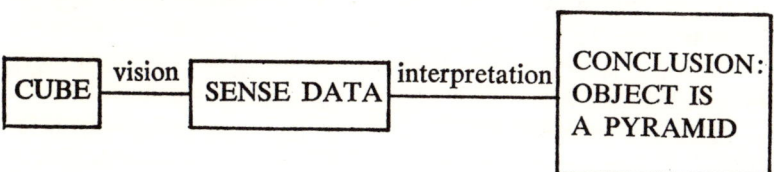

Obviously a mistake has been made. The question is, Where? In which phase of the process? Why, in the only phase that involves any judgment: in the *interpretation* phase.

A person's senses provide him with data that correspond to real objects. The person must develop the art of interpreting his sense data so that he can correctly decide what object a particular set of sense data corresponds to. If he makes a mistake, he must place the blame not on his senses but on his judgment. His senses function automatically and have no power of choice and therefore no ability to deceive him; his interpretive judgment, however, *is* fallible.

A person develops his interpretive skill through experience.

Suppose I am sitting at a dinner table and I look at a circular plate at the far end of the table. Because I am seeing the plate obliquely instead of looking directly down at it, the image on the retina of my eye is not a circle. Rather, its outline appears elliptical. From experience I can tell that the plate is actually circular. Nevertheless, the image in my mind is ellipitical. As a matter of fact, it has to be, as required by the laws of geometry and optics. If I were to conclude that the plate actually is ellipitical instead of circular, the fault would lie with my judgment, not with my senses. *They* were functioning properly in providing the sense data; *I* made the mistake in my evaluation of the sense data.

Another example: The sun and moon appear to be about the same size. They should: the sun, though much larger than the moon, is also much further away. My vision is functioning properly by producing equal images of sun and moon. If I were to conclude that they are in fact the same size, my judgment would be at fault, not my senses.

My senses provide my mind with sense data. It is my job to develop the skill of accurately interpreting such data. My senses work automatically and lack the power to misrepresent, but my judgment can be wrong.

In other words, to use your senses properly you must learn to correlate your sense data with the objects engendering the data.

This is a responsibility to yourself that you cannot afford to ignore. A person who claims, for instance, that his senses are deceiving him—that the image of a circular plate should always be circular regardless of the angle from which he views it—is complaining that his senses function in accordance with the laws of nature instead of functioning as he would like them to. His objection is that he has to adjust his evaluations to his senses, that his senses will not obligingly function as he wishes they would.

This is a tragically foolish attitude. As long as you are willing to rely on your senses, you can educate your evaluative judgment, which is the only phase of the process you have any control over:

senses		interpretation	
(function automatically)		(you can control this)	

However, a person who refuses to accept the validity of his senses will be powerless to use them properly.

Let's speak plainly. In order to live, a man must learn about the world around him. His senses provide the raw data for his mind to use in the effort to sustain his life. The issue of accepting or rejecting the validity of one's senses is, in the long run, the issue of life or death.

This is not to deny that our perceptual range is limited. For instance: some things are too small to see, some pitches are too high to hear, a change in temperature may be too slight to feel. Often we must build instruments like microscopes to assist us. Nevertheless, we must first accept the validity of our senses; it is only through our senses that we can perceive anything an instrument can tell us.

It may be objected that senses do sometimes distort. What about optical illusions and color blindness? Aren't these instances of our senses deceiving us?

No.

We are fooled by an optical illusion because it presents an arrangement of lines and shapes which is not familiar. Lacking experience with such a pattern, and drawing upon the experience we do have (which is not suitable for the occasion), we make a swift but incorrect evaluation of what we see.

A color-blind person sees things differently from people who are not color-blind. When two colors appear the same to him, they may in fact be different. But again, his senses are not deceiving him. They are merely functioning consistently and automatically in a certain (atypical) way. The color-blind person must learn to interpret his sense data just as other people must learn to interpret theirs. The color-blind person's problems in sense interpretation may be special, but they are problems of judgment, not distortions by his sense of sight.

To a person with normal vision, salt looks just like sugar. Yet the two substances are actually quite different. Is his sense of sight unreliable? Or must he simply learn that in many cases it is necessary to investigate further than visual appearances before drawing any conclusions?

Although most of our examples have dealt with the sense of sight, examples could be found for the other senses as well, the principle remaining exactly the same: my senses provide me with data; what use I make of the data is up to me.

The idea that the senses are unreliable is an extremely destructive notion. If your senses, your channels of information from the outside world, were unreliable, then all knowledge would be futile, resting on an unreliable base. Since you must learn about the world outside yourself in order to live effectively, your ability to sustain your life would be seriously impaired indeed.

No wonder, then, that a person who accepts this doctrine is likely to feel inadequate to the task of living. He will lack intellectual confidence, and his joy in living will be meager. How can it be otherwise, when he believes that he cannot depend upon his only source of data about the universe of which he is a part? A feeling of helplessness is not conducive to happiness.

Such a person is easy prey for those who traffic in mysticism and faith. Believing that he cannot rely solely on his natural faculties, and feeling helpless as a result, he may choose to accept the "supernatural" revelations of religious teachers as a substitute for knowledge.

Or such a person may turn to "consciousness-expanding"

drugs. While hallucinogenic drugs *change* the manner in which a person's senses function, that is not the same as *improving* sense perception. Indeed, the drug user is handicapped, as we shall now see.

We have noted that it is essential for a person to learn to interpret his sense data. This means that he must be familiar with the manner in which his senses function (and clearheaded enough to make interpretive judgments). Therefore, anything that makes his senses function in an unfamiliar manner makes it harder, not easier, for him to interpret his sense data. He is at a disadvantage because his manner of interpreting sense data under normal conditions does not square off with the sense data he receives when he is in the unfamiliar state.

A pilot flying in a fog can rely on instruments to help him make a safe landing. But suppose his instruments have been tampered with. Will it be easier or harder for him to make a safe landing?

Drugs (and alcohol) tamper with one's sensory apparatus, and therefore handicap one. Things seem very unusual to a person in a drugged state, but that doesn't make his perceptions better; it only makes them different. And that makes it harder, not easier for him, to make intelligent judgments.

(What is being said here should not be taken as a blanket endorsement of present narcotics laws. We are considering the effects of drugs on the individual, and not addressing ourselves to a social question. The social side will be covered in Part Three.)

Even if a person were to become accustomed to the unusual perceptions of the drugged state and to develop some skill in interpreting his sense data in that condition, he would gain nothing. Seeing the world differently is not the same as seeing it better. And after a sufficient time the wild effects of the drug would become as commonplace for such a person as what the rest of us see is to us. Senses function by providing us with information, not necessarily thrills.

"Consciousness-expanding" drugs expand nothing. They do not assist our senses, as a microscope does, but rather tamper with our senses—and who needs that? (A microscope is used in conjunction with the sense of sight; it does not pervert the visual apparatus.)

People tempted to use such drugs habitually should consider the possible medical effects.

They should also ask themselves whether they have had confidence in their senses and have made full use of them. Our senses are wonderful faculties, capable of giving us much knowledge—and pleasure, too. They should not be sold short.

4 Concepts

Looking back at what we have considered so far, we can recall certain points:

1. By the Law of Causality the actions of a thing follow from its nature. What it is determines how it acts.

2. Applied to living things, the Law of Causality indicates that every organism has, according to its nature, a proper manner of living. This manner requires that the organism use its full powers, in expression of its full nature.

3. Man, being a living organism, also has a proper manner of living, the key to which is determined by his highest powers.

4. Unlike lower forms of life, man is not programmed by his nature to act automatically in his own best interest. By his power of choice a man can (and, alas, often does) act in a way that is contrary to the requirements of successful living. Hence it is vital to understand what man's proper manner of living is so that we can then *choose* to adopt it in our lives.

Our task now is to examine man's special powers to learn how they should be used to sustain and further our lives. We'll begin by considering the faculty of reason.

Reason is the faculty that assimilates a man's sense data.

Once perceived and identified, the knowledge can be related to and combined with other knowledge (integrated). This ability to identify and integrate sense data is man's alone. No other known form of life has it.

The central operation of reason is concept-formation.[1]

---

[1] The ideas we are now considering are set forth in Ayn Rand's book *Introduction to Objectivist Epistemology,* published in 1967 by The Objectivist, Inc. This treatment of the Objectivist theory of knowledge (epistemology) was originally published in eight installments in the *Objectivist* magazine, July, 1966, through Feb., 1967.

Suppose I see some triangles. I notice several things:

1. The triangles all have a distinguishing characteristic: they are all three-sided.

2. Each triangle has certain measurements: lengths of sides, sizes of angles.

I can now form the concept "triangularity" in this way:

3. I mentally isolate the distinguishing characteristic (three-sidedness).

4. At the same time I omit from my mind any specific measurements.

"Triangularity" as a concept contains the idea of three-sidedness but does not specify any definite measurements. I know that a particular triangle must have definite measurements (lengths of sides and sizes of angles), but because these measurements vary from triangle to triangle they are not specified in the concept. In this way the concept is general and refers to any and all triangles.

This example illustrates the process by which concepts are formed. Because concept-formation is so natural to us, we don't often take notice of the separate steps in the process. These steps, enumerated in the last example, are as follows:

1. Two or more units (things) are observed to share some *distinguishing characteristic(s)*.

2. The units being observed are measurable in various ways, and the *measurements* differ from one unit to the next.

3. By a process called *abstraction* the mind isolates the common aspect of the units: the distinguishing characteristic(s).

4. At the same time the mind omits the variable aspect of the units: the measurements.

No set of measurements is contained in the concept because no one set is more significant than any other. A triangle whose sides are 3, 4, and 5 is no more or less triangular than one whose sides measure 12.1, 15.9, and 20.6.

A concept is general because it is (*a*) based upon one or more distinguishing characteristics common to the units being considered, while at the same time (*b*) free of any particular measurements that differ from unit to unit. Some additional examples follow.

When I handle several different objects, I notice that (1) they all have the property of weight, while (2) the amount of weight varies from one object to the next. (This much I grasp perceptually, even if I don't know how to measure weight with instruments like scales or balances.) In my mind I (3) isolate the property of weight, while (4) omitting any specific amount of weight, since the amount varies from object to object. In this way, the concept of "weight" is formed in my mind.

I see moving objects and observe (1) the similarity of their activity (change of position), and also note that (2) the measurement of this activity (how fast? what direction?) is variable. Mentally isolating the activity (3), while omitting specific measurements of speed and direction (4), I arrive at the concept of "motion."

I observe many human beings and note certain distinguishing characteristics (living, biped, two-eyed, rational, speaking, etc., etc.). I also note that these qualities differ from man to man: one man is tall, another is short; one is more intelligent than another; etc. Isolating the distinguishing characteristics (of which there are too many to list fully here) while omitting measurements, I arrive at the concept of "man."

A concept contains all that you know about the units the concept refers to. As you learn more the new knowledge becomes part of your concept. Concepts can always receive new data, and in fact must be open to updating. This is because concepts are formed in the context of your knowledge and experience, which themselves are constantly expanding.

(The treatment of concept-formation given here far from exhausts the topic. We have not considered, for instance, how concepts are combined to form a new, wider concept, nor how a concept can be subdivided into new, narrower concepts. The manner in which we widen or subdivide our concepts is interesting, but to discuss it would take us too far afield. This topic is covered in Miss Rand's book on epistemology.)

It may be asked, Exactly what significance is there to all this? In what way is concept-formation important to man in his effort to live successfully?

Concept-formation is of profound and crucial importance to us. Here is why: Your range of consciousness is limited. You can think of only so much at any given time. For instance, to think simultaneously of all the human beings you've ever seen would be impossible. But the concept of "man," as a single object of thought, can be held before your consciousness, bringing into awareness all the vast data it contains, all the essentials you know about man.

This is the tremendous value of concepts. A concept is a single unit of thought that refers to many individual units. As such it condenses knowledge into an intellectually manageable unit of thought, thereby giving new scope to your range of consciousness. A concept like "man" stands for the countless individuals it refers to, and contains all the essential aspects of mankind you know of, while not containing any specific details of measurement. Stripped of variables of measurement, the concept is a streamlined package of knowledge for you to use in your effort to effectively sustain and forward your life.

Concepts are needed for any distinctively human activity, from arithmetic to heart-transplant surgery, from writing a thank-you note to writing the United States Constitution, from planning tonight's supper to formulating the theory of relativity. Concepts are used by thinking men to reshape their environment and advance their lives—and the lives of many around them.

We use concepts by forming them into chains of thought according to rules derived from the laws of existence, rules called *logic*—our next topic of discussion.

5 Logic

Consider the following two statements:
1. All trees have roots.
2. All oaks are trees.

Assuming that these two statements are correct, what conclusion can you draw from them? It is:

3. All oaks have roots.

This is a simple example of logical reasoning, by which new knowledge is derived from previous knowledge. Given the first two statements, called premises, which represent facts already known to him, the reasoner is able to arrive at a new fact, the conclusion. This is the immense value of logic: it enables us to expand our knowledge.

Now, try this: Assuming that you accept the two premises, see whether you can avoid coming to the indicated conclusion. A moment's reflection will show you that it is quite impossible to escape the conclusion if you accept the premises.

Why does the conclusion follow so inexorably from the premises? Before answering that question we must consider a more basic one: What justifies the making of statements like 1 and 2 in the first place?

The meaningfulness of such premises depends upon the Law of Identity: Whatever exists has a specific nature.

Consider, for example, the first premise above: All trees have roots. This statement indicates that (*a*) a tree, as an entity, has a specific nature, and (*b*) rootedness is part of that nature. In other words, the making of the statement presupposes that a tree is a specific kind of thing, having a definite nature; the statement itself asserts something *about* that nature.

This example illustrates the principle that any statement telling what a thing is (or what attributes it has or actions it performs) rests ultimately on the Law of Identity. First, a thing has a definite nature; then, an aspect of that nature can be identified in a statement.

The same is true of negative statements—those that deny rather than affirm. For example, the statement "No man is a mineral" tells us that (*a*) a man has a specific nature, (*b*) a mineral has a specific nature, and (*c*) these natures are different. Any statement that an entity is *not* something rests on the fact that it *is* something else. Hence even negative statements depend on the Law of Identity.

The Law of Identity justifies the mental operation of forming assertions about things. That is not to say that every assertion we can possibly make is correct. The statement "A horse has five legs" appears to assert something about the true nature of horses. But it happens that a horse has four legs, not five. The statement that a horse has five legs does not agree with reality, and is therefore designated as false. The statement "All trees have roots," which agrees with reality, is true. The Law of Identity justifies in principle our making statements about things, but any particular statement must be tested against the facts of reality to determine whether it is true or not.

It should be noted that an assertion may be neither true nor false. For example, the statement "Another world war will begin in the year 2000" predicts an event. Perhaps the event will occur; perhaps not. In any case the events of the year 2000 lie in the future and are therefore quite indefinite at this moment. Since the truth or falsity of a statement depends upon whether it agrees with or contradicts reality, and since the history of the year 2000 is, as yet, indefinite and undecided, it follows that the prediction itself is neither true nor false at this time. A statement cannot be true or false unless the alleged facts it refers to are actualized in reality. A statement that is either true or false is called a *proposition*.

Much more can be said about propositions—and about the entire subject of logic—than will be covered in this book. Our treatment of logic here has a special viewpoint and purpose: we

Logic

wish to show that the operations and rules of logic follow from the laws of existence, and are not arbitrary conventions, as is sometimes claimed. (Readers seeking a complete treatment of logic will find a number of texts on the subject.)

We have already seen that proposition-formation is in fact justified by a basic law of existence. The same is true of reasoning, the linking of propositions into chains of thought, like the one we used to begin this discussion:

1. All trees have roots.
2. All oaks are trees.
3. Therefore all oaks have roots.

The reason the conclusion follows inevitably from the premises is that the laws of existence require it; the rules of logic are merely applications of these laws.

To see this better, let's try to form a different conclusion about the rootedness of oaks (while retaining the same two premises), and see what happens. Since the conclusion (3) states that all oaks have roots, any different conclusion about the rootedness of oaks would have to claim that not all oaks have roots—that at least some (if not all) oaks are rootless. Therefore, in place of conclusion 3, we'll substitute the following:

3a. Some oaks do not have roots.

This gives a new chain of "reasoning":

1. All trees have roots.
2. All oaks are trees.
3a. Therefore some oaks do not have roots.

Since statement 2 tells us that oaks are trees, we would be justified is referring to oaks by the more general name "trees." We now make this substitution of "trees" for "oaks" in statement 3a:

3a. Some trees do not have roots.

Now, juxtapose this with premise 1:

1. All trees have roots.
3a. Some trees do not have roots.

These statements allege that while all trees do have roots (statement 1), some trees do not (statement 3a). But we know a law of existence that forbids such a state of affairs. Remember?

"Existence and non-existence are mutually exclusive." A thing either is or is not; it can't be both ways. An oak tree either has roots or does not; it can't be both ways. Since this basic axiom of existence (called the Law of Non-Contradiction) would be contradicted by conclusion 3a, we must reject 3a, as not following from 1 and 2.

Normally, of course, we don't consciously check out reasoning against the laws of existence as we have done here. It seems obvious to us that 3a does not follow from 1 and 2, and this is a tribute to our rational faculty, so well developed as to be automatized, saving us the trouble of consciously having to refer back to the laws of existence every time we think. But it is well to be aware that our laws of thought, as they are sometimes called, are in fact applications of the axioms of existence itself.

When we sought a different conclusion to substitute for "All oaks have roots," we naturally selected one that contained the idea that not all oaks have roots (and then saw why this conclusion is wrong). Have we now considered all the statements that could be proposed as possible conclusions for premises 1 and 2? Or does there remain some alternative, another possible conclusion about oaks and roots, one that neither affirms nor denies that every oak has roots? It would be profitable for the reader to answer this question for himself (by referring back to the law that existence and non-existence are jointly exhaustive), and to satisfy himself that for premises 1 and 2, statement 3 is the conclusion demanded by reality—and therefore by the rules of logic.

Is it possible to observe the rules of logic and still arrive at a false conclusion? Yes, as in this case:
    All birds are fish.
    Crows are birds.
    Therefore crows are fish.
The logic of this reasoning is not at fault, but the first premise is clearly wrong. The falsity of the first premise accounts for a false conclusion being reached even though the rules of logic are observed. Logic yields true conclusions so long as the premises are true to begin with. If ever you seem to get a wrong answer although your logic is sound, follow the often-quoted advice given

in *Atlas Shrugged:* Check your premises. At least one of them is wrong.

The preceding discussion illustrates but a few of the rules of logic, and is intended to give the reader a glimpse of the connection between the laws of existence and the laws of thought. Pseudophilosophical attacks on the validity of thought and logic are not exactly unheard of. Hence it is crucial to appreciate the fact that the principles of human thought are sanctioned by reality itself.

By the art of logic we are able to expand our knowledge of reality by identifying previously unknown facts. But in identifying these facts we must be guided by the laws of existence so as never to arrive at a contradiction of any kind. Since contradictions don't exist, it is only through error that one can arrive at contradictory ideas, and only through checking one's reasoning and premises that the error can be found and corrected.

In our simple example of reasoning we dealt with only three concepts: "tree," "oak," and "rootedness." Such an example gives but an infinitesimal idea of the value of logic and the manner in which logic, applied to concepts, expands our knowledge. Even to list, let alone analyze, the instances of reasoning in our everyday lives would be an enormous task, as the reader can see for himself if he tries to recollect all the ways in which he practices logical thought from day to day. And the systematic and intensive application of logic in science, art, and business has reshaped the earth, providing man with uncountable benefits.

Concept-formation and logical thought are key functions of the faculty of reason and are therefore crucial to human life. But one's rational faculty does not work automatically. A man has the power of choice; if he is to think (and therefore live), he must *choose* to think. We must now consider the power of choice in human consciousness.

6 Volitional Consciousness

Volition (or free will) has to do with man's reason—with his faculty of conceptual awareness, as opposed to his sensory-perceptual awareness. As we have seen, the latter faculty is common to all animal life, while reason is man's alone.

To understand the exact nature of volition we must consider two main points.

1. The sharpness of a man's rational awareness varies at different times and in different situations. For each individual there are many different levels of awareness, on any one of which his reason can operate.

An example will illustrate this. Suppose I am sitting in my room, relaxing. My mind is not focused on anything in particular; we may say that it is operating on a fairly low level of rational awareness. As I glance around the room my eyes come to a picture on the wall. Something about the picture is distracting. What is it? With a slight increase in my level of awareness I recognize what it is about the picture that caught my attention: the picture is crooked. At a still higher level of awareness I may consider the problem of how to adjust the picture so that it will hang straight. Finally I may see a solution: I can move a chair up next to the wall so that I can then stand on the chair to reach and straighten the picture. Whether or not I actually proceed to do so, the problem of the crooked picture has been solved to the extent that my mind has conceived a plan of corrective action.

Note that my mind's level of awareness increased at several points in pursuing the train of thought about the crooked picture. Branden cities (4/64, 15) three indicators of increased rational awareness: increased clarity of the mind's contents (such as consciously identifying the disturbing aspect of the picture); greater degree of abstract thinking ("crookedness" is a geometric-esthetic concept); placing the object of thought in a wider, relevant context (such as seeing something else in the room—the chair—as an implement to assist in adjusting the picture).

In brief, there is a whole spectrum of rational awareness possible to a man. But what determines the level on which a man's mind does function in a given situation? This brings us to the second main point:

2. Generally speaking, a man's level of awareness at any given moment is regulated by the man himself.

Here is the essence of volition. A man has the power to choose to raise or lower his level of awareness (within his limits), to focus or defocus his mind, to regulate the action of his own consciousness (1/64, 3).

Of course, the man must be on *some* level of consciousness before he can make this choice; he cannot, for example, be asleep or otherwise unconscious, for then he could not choose anything at all (4/64, 15).

In the previous example I chose to identify the disturbing aspect of the picture; I didn't have to. Then I chose to consider the problem of adjusting the picture; I didn't have to. I persevered until a plan of corrective action was formulated; I didn't have to. At any point I could have dropped the whole subject by lowering my level of awareness.

Objectivism identifies man's power of choice as his power to regulate his level of conceptual awareness. Several observations on this point follow.[1]

Recalling the distinction between sensory-perceptual awareness (animals have this) and conceptual awareness (only man has this), the first point to be made is that, as capabilities, both are implanted by nature. The difference being considered here is in the exercising of these capabilities. A man's sensory-perceptual apparatus operates automatically. On the other hand, his conceptual

---

[1] A thorough explanation of volition is given by Branden in a two-part article in the *Objectivist*, Jan. and Feb. 1966.

faculty—reason—operates only by his choice in any given situation. Confronted with any problem, large or small, a man may or may not adjust his level of awareness to an appropriate level to deal with the problem. (That is not to say, of course, that if he does choose to think about it he will necessarily solve the problem; his success or failure will depend upon his knowledge of the factors in the problem. The choice to think does not result in infallibility.)

The choice to focus or defocus one's mind is a "casual primary." In other words, it is not a reaction to any previous influences on the person. Rather, the person himself is the cause of his choice. This is in keeping with the Law of Causality: what a thing is determines how it can act. A living thing can, as we have seen, initiate its own actions. As a special case of this general principle, a man is able, by his own power, to make the choice to think or not. The need to make the choice is imposed by man's nature; which choice he actually makes in any given situation is up to him (3/66, 9-13).

Note that the content of a man's thoughts does depend on prior factors: his knowledge, interests, values, etc. Hence the choice of *what* to think about is not a causal primary. But the choice of *whether* to think is. It is up to the individual to direct his mind to think, to grasp, to question, to examine the validity of previous thinking, and to sustain mental focus as needed.

Many people think of volition or free will exclusively in terms of actions. Volition, they say, means that a man can *act* as he chooses, within the limits of what is possible to him. This is true, but only indirectly. The power of choice pertains directly to thought. But a man's actions follow from his thoughts. Therefore, since his mind is volitional, his actions—which come from his mind—are, derivatively, also volitional. That is why a man is responsible for his actions. It is not that they are under the direct control of his will, but rather that they are controlled by his mind, which *is* volitional.

It should be stressed that a man cannot permanently commit himself to think. He must decide anew in each new situation. However, a man who habitually chooses to exercise his rational

Volitional Consciousness

ability is able to do so with less effort than his less rational neighbor.

On the other hand, it is possible for a man to habitually evade the act of focusing his mind. Evasion involves a choice to shrink one's awareness, and thereby entails a sabotaging of the mind by its owner.

Habitual evasion puts a man at a serious disadvantage in life. As we have seen, man's survival depends upon his exercising his faculty of reason; this is why most people sense that they *should* think. But many choose to evade instead, being unwilling to exert the effort needed to focus the mind, or to face unpleasant facts, or to sacrifice the indulgence of whims. Whatever the motive, a man's deliberate holding down of his rational faculty puts him in a position roughly analogous to that of a bird with a broken wing. The crucial difference is that a bird would never set about to break its own wing. A bird lacks the power of choice and is programmed by nature to act in its own best interest. Only man is in the position of being able to sabotage his own survival faculty by his own choice.

Suppose that, through some grotesque biological malfunction, a bird actually set about to break its own wings. Think about what your reaction would be upon witnessing such a thing. And then think about a human being sabotaging his most vital faculty, not through biological malfunction, but by his own free choice.

Horrifying, isn't it?

7 Values

Because reason is man's basic tool of survival, and because reason functions only by choice, it follows that to live successfully, a man must choose to think. But that is not all he has to do in order to live. Obviously a man who did nothing but think would soon starve. Remember that life involves self-sustaining *action,* and although thinking is the most fundamental and crucial of life-serving actions, a man must perform a great many additional actions in order to survive. The sequence of events from thinking to other life-serving action is as follows:

1. First, a man must choose to exercise his reason in any and every situation. In this way he learns from experience. He forms concepts and draws logical conclusions about himself and his environment.

2. On the basis of his thinking he comes to regard certain things as good for him (i.e., as necessary or useful to his life). He also comes to regard certain other things as bad for him (harmful to his life). Quite a few things seem neutral (neither good nor bad). He further realizes that it is necessary for him to perform various actions if he is to obtain the beneficial things and avoid the harmful ones.

3. Consequently he acts to get, keep, use, or enjoy the things he regards as good for him, and to shun (or destroy if necessary) the things he regards as harmful.

The things that a man acts to gain and/or keep are his *values* (5/66, 1), while those that he seeks to avoid or eliminate can be called *disvalues*. Using these terms, we can restate the pattern of human survival this way: By choosing to think, a man learns about himself and his environment, selecting values (and disvalues) accordingly. Understanding that the attaining of values (and the

Values

avoiding of disvalues) requires action, he proceeds to undertake such action as and when appropriate.

This is the most vital conclusion so far in our inquiry into the nature of man and his life. We now consider this conclusion in greater detail.

In the first place a man needs to act in order to live. Therefore he needs values, toward which his actions will be directed. He has no choice about the need for values, only about what his values will be.

Furthermore, reality—including his nature as a human being—must be accommodated if he is to survive. Reality places certain demands upon him, and he can ignore these demands only at his own peril. For instance, a man who does not eat will die, and that's that. Remember, at all times, that reality always has the last word. Hence it is not enough that a man merely select values; he must select correct values—correct as measured against reality.

Finally, since reason is man's tool of cognition, by which he learns about reality and its demands, it follows that his values are to be derived through his exercise of reason.

It should be understood that the actions being discussed here include only those under volitional control. We do not include pulse, respiration, digestion, reflexes, and other such operations, since they occur automatically. Not all life-serving actions are volitional, but in this discussion we are concerned only with those that are.

As noted earlier, the values a man selects must be correct—consonant with reality. That a man selects something as a value does not prove that it is good for him. A man can err in defining what is good for him. Moreover, as we have seen, he can evade his responsibility to think, thereby arriving at his values by whim or in some other irrational way. But never forget that the purpose of a set of values is to enable a man to act in a way that actually *will* further his life, not merely to act in a way that he *wishes* would further it. A man who eats poison while wishing it were food will end up just as dead. To repeat: reality always has the last word.

An important feature of a man's value code is that it is not merely a collection of values but a *hierarchy* of values. Just as a man comes to regard certain things as values, he comes to regard some values as greater than others. Not all things are valued equally. If a man finds that he must choose between two values because circumstances do not permit him to have both, then his only rational course of action is to choose the greater value. For instance, if a man is fond of a certain kind of food, but his physician advises him against eating it, then the man will abstain (assuming that he values his continued health more than the pleasure of eating the food). It is irrational ever to sacrifice a greater value for a lesser one; to do so is to act against reason because it was reason that assigned each value to its place in the hierarchy. Such irrational action requires deliberate evasion of one's knowledge, deliberate suspension of thought. (This does not mean, of course, that a man may not *rearrange* his hierarchy of values, provided he does so through rational reconsideration.)

It is extremely important for a man to consciously develop his code of values, to know what his values are and what their hierarchical arrangement is. For it often happens that a man finds himself in a situation that calls for a quick decision. In such a situation he will not have time to reason out his code of values. It is imperative, therefore, that a man formulate his code in advance—at his leisure, so to speak—so that he can act quickly when the need arises. In short, he must plan ahead.

A man's values are great in number and cover a wide spectrum, from the essentials of life to those myriad things that add joy and color to the experience of living—or should. A man's choice of values is crucial to him, for, as the goals of his every chosen act, they are the life of life itself.

8 Reason, Purpose, Self-Esteem

In forming his value code, a man has virtually unlimited choice as to what his values will be and what hierarchical arrangement they will have. Nevertheless, we can show that there are certain things that a man must include among his supreme values if he is to live successfully.

First on the list, of course, is reason itself. As we have seen, reason is man's cognitive link with the universe, his highest power, and his basic tool of survival. It follows that a man must value reason above all else if he is really interested in living the life of a man.

But besides reason, there are two other values of supreme importance. We'll approach one of these by way of an analogy—an analogy with the game of chess.

In chess each of the two players has a set of pieces: King, Queen, Rooks, Bishops, Knights, and Pawns. These pieces can be moved on a chessboard in various ways according to fixed rules. The object of the game is to checkmate (trap) your opponent's King by suitable placement of your own pieces on the board. In other words, checkmate is your long-range goal. But it is not possible to achieve checkmate on your first move of the game. Rather, there will be a long sequence of moves, alternating between you and your opponent, and you must play so as to lead up to your objective. During the game, therefore, you pursue a series of short-range goals, such as capturing (removing from play) various opposing pieces. Each of these intermediate goals serves as a means to ultimate end: checkmate. Capturing some of your opponent's pieces, for instance, weakens his position and makes it harder for him to defend his King—which is what you're after. (It also makes it harder for him to attack your own King.) A good chess player's every move is geared ultimately to the achievement of his objective.

But of course, before you can play toward an objective, you must first know what it is.

Suppose you sat down to play a game of chess, knowing how each piece moves and captures, but not knowing the object of the game—not knowing that your purpose is to checkmate your opponent's King. How would you proceed to play? What moves could you make? If you were strictly rational about it, you could not make even one move, because you would have no way of knowing whether a particular move would serve or hinder your unknown objective. For example, you might consider moving out a Knight as your opening move; but for all you knew, the object of the game might be to capture one's opponent's Knights—in which case moving out one of your own Knights could be dangerous. Clearly you could not make a single, rational move without first knowing the ultimate objective.

So it is with any undertaking. First you have a purpose in view; then you perform an action or sequence of actions aimed at achieving the purpose. Only when you have a purpose in mind can you then reason out your course of action, choosing your actions according to how well they serve your purpose.

This same necessity for purpose applies (in the extreme) to the activity of living. A man needs a purpose in life—that is, a set of long-range goals around which he organizes his life and for the sake of which he performs the necessary short-range actions of day-to-day living. Living without a purpose is like sailing without a compass. Without a purpose in life a man is like someone trying to play chess without knowing the object of the game, moving pieces at random, not knowing from one minute to the next what he is doing or where he is heading. Such a man lives in a motivational chaos, acting from moment to moment, to achieve this value or that, his life a crazy quilt, a conglomeration of fragments which do not fit together to form any whole because they aren't unified by a purpose.

In chess the objective is fixed by the rules of the game. In life the objective is chosen by the person himself. His choice will depend on his abilities, aptitudes, knowledge—the whole context of his life. He may choose to write plays, fly airplanes, operate a store, be an athlete or a carpenter or a scientist—or a rebel. The choice is his to make. But without a purpose he is not living the life of a man.

In chess, once the objective is achieved the game is over. In life the achievement of one's purpose is an ongoing thing. A man doesn't become a writer so that he can write one book and then stop. Nor does a man open a business just so that he can close it a week later. Purpose is essential to life, and must be as enduring.

There is one more supreme value that a man needs in order to live: the conviction that he can and should live, the conviction that he is competent and worthy to live.

First: A man must be aware that he has the ability to live, that the struggle of living is not beyond him. No one attempts something unless he believes that success is possible, and a man will not make the effort to live if he feels that he is doomed to fail. Hence, if he is to live successfully, a man must realize that he has the ability to do so. Otherwise his attitude will be, Why should I bother?

Second: A man must consider himself worthy of life. If he regards himself as depraved or evil, for instance, he will not be motivated to pursue values or work toward a purpose in life. Again, his attitude will be, Why should I bother? If a man is to perform the purpose-directed, value-winning actions of living, then he must value the beneficiary of such actions: himself (Branden: 3/67, 4). Just as you don't act in behalf of someone else unless you value him, so you won't act for your own sake unless you value yourself.

These two elements—confidence in your ability to live and conviction of your worthiness to live—blend to form the value called self-esteem. We'll have more to say about self-esteem in a later chapter. For now, let it be understood that self-esteem is a ratification in one's mind of two *facts* of reality; it is a realization that one's ability and one's worthiness to live are indeed facts to be accepted, not groundless hopes. These facts are as follows.

A man has the ability to live because he has the faculty of reason (as well as his lesser powers), and there is ample evidence that reason is efficacious, that it works. This evidence is to be seen by an individual not only in his own achievements but in human progress in general. The awareness, the realization, that he is equipped with an efficacious tool of survival is one of the two roots of a man's self-esteem.

As to the other root, his worthiness to live: A man's very existence sanctions his struggle for life. He is worthy of living because if he were not, he could not exist in the first place. Of the man who cries, "I am not fit to live," we can ask, "Then how do you explain the fact that you *do* live?" Reality has deemed that he does exist, and this is all the sanction a man needs (or should want): the sanction of reality itself.

Perhaps these things seem obvious. Yet for centuries philosophies have been put forth attacking and denying the efficacy of reason and the objective worthiness of man. And this vast and ancient assault on self-esteem continues today. For a man to achieve and keep this crucial value in a culture beset by such blatant irrationality, it is imperative that he arm himself intellectually with an understanding of what self-esteem is, why it is a value, and how it is justified.

9 *Morality*

We have considered such topics as volition, action, values, value codes, and purpose in life. There is a concept which deals with these topics: the concept of "morality."

But what is morality? From common usage we know that this word pertains to the topics mentioned above, and that it does so from a particular viewpoint: that of good vs. evil (or right vs. wrong). This poses yet another riddle: What do the words "good" and "evil" really mean? There have been many attempts to define them; ideas on the nature of good and evil are set forth in various religious, political, and social theories. The good has been proclaimed as being that which pleases God, serves society, or advances a revolution. It will not be necessary for us to dwell on such theories, for we are in a position to reason out a valid standard of morality, that is, of good and evil.

Looking back, we can recall that man, like other organisms, faces the alternative of life or death; and that man, unlike other organisms, can survive only by choosing to think. It is this choice that underlies all the other choices a man can make. Note that such considerations as values and purpose arise only as a consequence of the choice to live. Bearing in mind the fundamentality of the life-death alternative, we can arrive at the concepts of good and evil. The life-serving is the good (the moral), while the life-negating is the evil (immoral).

Life is the standard of morality.

We can easily show that any other standard of morality is unsound: To the extent that such a standard ever demands action inimical to life (or forbids action favorable to life), it forces a man to choose between "being good" on the one hand and acting in behalf of his life on the other. Life is enough of a struggle without having any life-serving things branded as evil or any harmful things glorified as good. Only by equating the morally good with the life-serving can we avoid such inconsistency.

Another point: It is by means of reason that a man decides *how* to perform moral (life-serving) action. It is through reason that a man forms his moral code, that is his code of values. Hence, man's moral faculty is none other than reason itself.

The rational and the moral are one.

It is not hard to show that any system of morality based on something other than reason is false: To the extent that such a system ever demands irrational action (or forbids rational action), it forces a man to choose between "being good" on the one hand, and being guided by his survival faculty on the other. By equating the moral with the rational, we preclude any clash between the two.

The information contained above can be summarized as follows:

Life-serving = rational = morally good
Life-negating = irrational = morally evil

This concept of morality is far removed from popular ideas on the subject. In fact, so many absurd and ugly connotations have become attached to the word morality that it seemed advisable to postpone the introduction and use of the word until after the basics of moral philosophy had been discussed. Those basics were discussed in recent chapters, while the word itself is used for the first time in the present chapter. But the common fallacies concerning morality are too widespread and too damaging to be ignored, and for this reason we now undertake some philosophical-sewage disposal.

First of all, many people think that morality rests on a religious or otherwise mystical base. Hence they regard reason and morality as conflicting standards between which they must choose. They feel that a completely rational person cannot be consistently moral, and vice versa. But as we have seen, the rational and the moral are one; there is no conflict, no need to choose between the two, no way to have one without the other.

Then there's the widespread idea that morality is a social concept. It isn't. The question is asked whether a man alone on a desert island would need morality. He definitely would. With no one else there to tell him what to do, he would have to exercise his mind to the fullest in order to survive. In other words, he would have to live by means of his reason—and that's what morality is all about.

This is not to deny that a social context raises many special moral questions (which will be dealt with in Part Three). Nevertheless, the plain fact is that, existentially and logically, *the concept of morality precedes the concept of society.* (That is why we have been able to develop the concept of morality without assuming or implying *any* social context.)

Another misconception is that morality is impractical, that a truly moral man is an impractical one, while a practical man must at times be immoral. But the standard of morality is life; therefore, if you want to practice life, morality *is* practical—as practical as engineering is to an astronaut.

If it seems hard to believe that the moral is the practical, it is because so many false notions have been preached in the name of morality that the image of morality itself has been damaged. (Examples: faith is superior to reason; it is better to compromise than to be divisive; it is holier to be poor than to be rich; planned parenthood is sinful, but baby farming is virtuous; Darwin may be right, but Genesis is sublime.) Such ideas represent fallacious codes of morality. Please remember that *we* are talking about the morality of reason whose standard is life— and you can't get more practical than that. The apparent breach between the practical and the moral is actually the very real breach between the practical and the immoral ideas that have been preached as moral.

It may seem to a few readers that the concept of morality presented here is that of hedonism: pleasure-seeking. Please note that our moral standard is life, not "pleasure." A fuller discussion of this point will be made when we discuss emotions. (See also 1/62, 7.) For the moment let it be noted that according to the philosophy we are developing, it is irrational (and therefore immoral) to pursue any pleasure unless the pursuit is compatible with one's life, values, and purpose.

Again, it may seem that the morality presented here asserts: Survive at any cost. But as we have stressed, mere animal survival is not sufficient or proper for man (see Chapter 2). Man's proper life is a life of reason, and this fact carries with it some important implications, one of which we discuss now.

When a man forms his heirarchy of values, some values will be so high that he will not want to live without them. They form the conditions or terms on which he chooses to live. These are the values whose loss would destroy his life psychologically as surely as starvation will destroy it physically. These are the values for which a man can morally risk his life—and perhaps die. (Note that a morality of "physical survival at any cost" could not logically justify such courses of action.)

A simple example of such a value is a man's reason itself, ideally his highest value. Would you care to go on living without your reason? Wouldn't you risk your life to prevent the loss of this value?

There are other possible examples. A man might risk his life to save his wife's, loving her so much that the prospect of living without her amply justifies the risk.

In extreme cases a man can morally choose a course of action leading to physical death. This does not contradict our premise that life is the standard of morality. Rather, it points up the fact that human life is more than mere animal survival, that survival without one's highest values is a living death. An example would be the case of a captured scientist who is willing to die rather than work for a government he despises. Faced with the prospect of using his mind to further the aims of a system he hates, he might well choose physical death as less repugnant than the living death, the psychological death, of placing his reason in the service of that which his reason identifies as evil.

One final thought: There are many unhappy people. Some even contemplate suicide. Such a person may actually be at the dead end of an irrational (and therefore life-negating) moral code. One reason why life can seem unbearable is that one is trying to live by a code that, though it may not be obvious, has something quite different from life at its root.

10 Duality of Awareness

Several chapters back we considered the relationship between a man's senses and his reason. We found that in response to things around him, a man's senses produce sense data, which can be identified and integrated by reason, resulting in the formation of concepts. We now consider two important implications of the relationship between man's senses and his reason.

1. As noted in chapter 4 (which the reader may wish to review at this time), through his power of concept-formation a man can distill the essential elements from a vast collection of sensory perceptions into a single concept, thereby tremendously increasing the scope of his consciousness. For example, your *per*ception of a man generates sense data containing many details of measurement. Your *con*cept of "man," on the other hand, contains only the essential information gleaned from many such perceptions. In this way the concept condenses knowledge into a manageable unit of thought, thereby allowing your mind to accomplish a great deal of thinking with a proportionately modest expenditure of effort. The following inference seems amply justified:

In terms of cognitive scope, the conceptual level of awareness is far superior to the perceptual.

2. On the other hand, please note that our direct cognitive contact with reality is furnished by our senses. Reason apprehends reality, not directly but through the intermediary of sense data. You may have in your mind an excellent concept of "man," but when you look around you it is not man you see; it is men: individual, concrete beings. This is not to deny that our concepts have validity, clarity, and certainty; the point being made here is that a concept is grasped in a way that is different from

the experiences of seeing, hearing, touching, tasting, and smelling. These latter experiences are unique in that they provide direct cognitive contact with reality. It should also be noted that our senses function automatically and effortlessly, while reason functions only by choice and with some degree of effort. We conclude as follows:

In terms of ease and directness of cognitive awareness, the perceptual level is superior to the conceptual.

This duality of awareness—the fact that we have two levels of consciousness, each having its own unique advantages—lies at the root of several patterns of human behavior. What happens is this: Because the perceptual mode of awareness is so direct and automatic, a man tends to value objects of perception which concretize his conceptual knowledge, so that he can apprehend such abstract knowledge with the ease and vividness of perception. In other words, he seeks to enjoy the advantages of the two modes of awareness simultaneously, in connection with the same object of thought. He can do this only by discovering (or creating) objects of perception which embody or symbolize his conceptual knowledge. Some examples follow.

One of the most important instances of concretization is the creation of language. A word is a perceptual symbol, but it refers back to a concept, thereby converting the concept into the mental equivalent of a concrete.

We create language in order to concretize our concepts.

By means of language a man can bring an abstract concept into sharp mental focus by merely recalling the concrete counterpart of the concept: the word.[1]

In creating a language, a man invents the concretes he needs (i.e., the words). In other instances of concretization a man simply seeks to find and perhaps possess some natural object which

---

[1] An interesting implication from the above discussion is that language is primarily a tool of cognition and only secondarily a tool of communication, so that an individual needs some kind of language to concretize his concepts even if he is not in a social context. For further discussion of this point see chap. 7 of *Introduction to Objectivist Epistemology*.

Duality of Awareness

concretizes a concept. Branden (12/67, 2) cites this example: Consider a family living in extreme poverty. They know conceptually that successful, prosperous life is possible, but there doesn't seem to be much concrete evidence of it. Such a family may seek concretization by acquiring a living, thriving organism. Branden suggests that this may be a partial explanation of the popularity of plants, say in window boxes, among such people; the sight of a thriving plant confirms on the perceptual level the concept that life can be successful.

Many additional examples of the concretization tendency can be found, and we'll be discussing some in upcoming chapters. Bear in mind that this tendency arises from the duality of awareness, which is a fact of human nature. Consequently, it is a fairly constant drive or yearning in man. Not everyone analyzes his mental operations, and no doubt many people are quite unaware of their tendency to concretize. (The impoverished family mentioned above would probably not understand fully why the window box seems so desirable.) But then, many people have only a limited understanding of the processes of concept-formation or logical reasoning, even though they use these processes every day. So it is with the concretization process: a seldom analyzed but ever-present feature of human consciousness.

11 Art

Many are the abstractions that man seeks to concretize, and many are the ways in which he does it. In this chapter we consider a way in which his most fundamental judgments are concretized.[1]

By a man's most fundamental judgment we mean here the judgments that form the link between his view of reality and his moral code. For example, in the early chapters of this book we reasoned out a number of such judgments:
— Man can know reality.
— Reason is his tool of cognition.
— Successful life is possible only through reliance on reason.
— Man has the power of choice, specifically, the power to think or not to think.

It was on the basis of such conclusions that we developed the fundamentals of a moral philosophy. Think how different a morality would follow from contrary conclusions. If, for instance, we insisted despite the evidence that reason is unreliable, faith is man's tool of cognition, man is evil by nature, and life on earth is only a penitential prelude to an afterlife, then we could not have arrived at a code of ethics that serves life through reason; it would instead serve death through faith. So it is that a man's fundamental judgments underlie his moral code.

The word "metaphysics" refers to the study of the fundamental nature of reality, and hence Ayn Rand designates these fundamental judgments as "metaphysical value-judgments."

One's metaphysical value-judgments follow from one's understanding (accurate or erroneous) of the nature of reality, and

---

[1] Most of this discussion was inspired by "The Psycho-Epistemology of Art" by Ayn Rand (4/65, 15 ff.).

one's code of ethics follows from those metaphysical value-judgments.

The question we now consider is this: How can man concretize such judgments? Remember that they are very wide in scope, dealing with the most fundamental issues facing man. What can concretize such concepts? Art.

In creating a work of art, the artist presents selected aspects of reality that concretize his metaphysical value-judgments: his conclusions about the fundamental relationship between man and reality. Some examples will make this clear.

In the realm of literature consider Ayn Rand's heroic characters, such as John Galt and Howard Roark, and consider the events in their lives. These are men of profound rationality, integrity, and self-esteem; they are purposeful, honest, independent, just, productive, and proud. And after much heroic effort they succeed and thrive, while villains like James Taggart and Peter Keating are destroyed. In her works Miss Rand has projected men who are moral ideals, and has proclaimed her judgment that such men are truly the best equipped to live, that evil is impotent.

By way of contrast consider now the philosophical viewpoint of William Golding's *Lord of the Flies*. In this work man (symbolized by boys cast away on an island) is seen as having an "essential illness"[2] which makes his rationality a fragile and fleeting thing and places him eternally on the brink of savagery. Evidently Golding's novel rests on metaphysical value-judgments quite different from those of Miss Rand. (Ayn Rand's novels, which depict man as noble and heroic, represent the school of *romantic* fiction.)

---

[2] Golding uses this phrase (not as part of dialogue) in chap. 5. It is worth noting that the phrase itself is a contradiction in terms. By the Law of Causality an organism has some normal mode of functioning which is a consequence of what the organism is, i.e., of its essence. Now, an illness is a departure from this normal mode of functioning—i.e., an illness is abnormal. Hence an essential illness would have to be some aspect of organic functioning which is simultaneously normal (because it's essential) and abnormal (because it's an illness)—clearly a contradiction. No illness can be essential, and nothing essential can be an illness.

In poetry we find concretizations of many diverse metaphysical estimates. Examples: that dumbfounded, ignorant wonder is preferable to scientific knowledge (Walt Whitman, "When I Heard the Learn'd Astronomer"); that a man cannot maintain his integrity (A. E. Housman, the twelfth of his *Last Poems*); or on the other hand, that the heroic courage and independent spirit is proper to man (W. E. Henley, "Invictus").

The visual arts can project man as glorious and noble (Greek sculpture) or depressing and ugly (Modigliani's paintings).

Make no mistake: behind every real work of art is a set of metaphysical value-judgments, valid or invalid. And art brings such judgments to the perceptual level of awareness so that they may be grasped as if they were concretes: it concretizes them.

Please note that the purpose of art is to concretize the artist's moral ideals, not to instruct the beholder in the philosophical basis of those ideals. Such instruction is the task of moral philosophy, not art. Art is not a substitute for such philosophy but rather a consequence of it.

Art does not teach; it shows. And that is what makes it so deeply important to a man.

12 The Subconscious

In discussing man's mind, we have considered only his conscious mental activity. There is, however, another side to the human mind: the subconscious. The subconscious mind can be understood more easily if we approach it through an analogy, an analogy with an electronic computer.

When a man needs a solution to a problem, he may use a computer to find it. He feeds the relevant data into the machine, which then integrates this information and supplies the needed result.

What enables the computer to integrate the data properly, so that the correct result is arrived at? The computer has been programmed in advance by the operator. This program is the sequence of operations that the machine is to perform on the data fed in. In other words, the program tells the computer what to do: when the operator feeds his data into the computer, it integrates the data according to the instructions contained in the program.

Why does a man use a computer at all? After all, the man already has the data needed to solve the problem (otherwise he couldn't feed it into the machine), and he knows how to get the answer from the data (otherwise he couldn't tell the machine how, via the program he writes for it). So why doesn't he do the job himself, say with pencil and paper, instead of resorting to an expensive computer? Because the computer can do the job much faster than the man could. The value of the computer lies largely in its speed. The operations performed by the computer take place so fast that even if they are displayed in some way to the operator as they occur, he cannot follow them. In addition the computer can store a lot more data than a man can hold in conscious focus.

In summary: a computer can store a tremendous amount of information and if properly programmed, can integrate it at very high speeds in order finally to supply a needed result.

Of course, a great deal depends on the program—the set of instructions given to the machine. If the program is not correct for the job to be done, then the results will not be, either.

The subconscious mind works like a computer. Like its electronic counterpart, the subconscious can store a great deal of information, integrate it at speeds too high for the conscious mind to follow, and supply results to the conscious mind. And like a computer it must be programmed. If programmed properly, it will function properly; if not, it will not. A computer is programmed by its operator; a man's subconscious is programmed by the man himself. The computer-like capabilities of the subconscious make it extremely important to a man. His subconscious can immensely aid (or tragically hinder) his life.

One example of how the subconscious works is found in creative thinking (8/66, 10). Suppose a scientist is trying to solve a problem. He has tried many approaches and failed. Then, quite suddenly—possibly while his conscious mind is occupied with other matters—an idea for a new approach to his problem comes to him out of the blue. He tries this new approach, and very possibly it succeeds. Such flashes of insight apparently result from subconscious integration. The scientist has programmed his subconscious to be on the alert in the area of his interest. Such programming is the result of his years of training and experience; it developed automatically, without his even being conscious of it. Consequently his subconscious mind can store and integrate countless pieces of data drawn from his observations and experiences—and can do this even while his conscious mind is otherwise occupied. And when the final connection has been made in the circuits of his subconscious, it signals the conscious mind.

Of course, such subconscious assistance is not restricted to scientists. Who has not had the experience at one time or another of suddenly being hit by an idea that proved valuable? The inspiration, the hunch that pays off—the roots of which seem im-

The Subconscious

possible to trace back afterward—these reflect benefits from the subconscious at work.

This example indicates some of the features of subconscious operation. The subconscious, as its name suggests, functions without conscious awareness, although the results of its functioning may be injected into consciousness (like a computer delivering an answer). Whether or not the results are useful depends on the programming. This programming, in turn, is not the result of a single act of the will. The subconscious is programmed slowly and cumulatively; a student beginning his study of science would not, other things being equal, achieve the same flash of insight as did the scientist in the previous example. And such programming is most likely specialized; even the most brilliant scientist will not necessarily experience such insights in areas unrelated to his work. A man's subconscious is programmed in many different ways, with many different degrees of efficiency; but then, many are the jobs it can do in a lifetime.

By way of contrast it is also possible to program one's subconscious to block the entrance of some thought into the conscious mind. The forbidden thought might be, for instance, a painful memory. Such unfortunate programming is called repression, of which more will be said later on.

These examples far from exhaust the set of subconscious operations. What we call intuition is certainly an instance of subconscious assistance to the conscious mind. Less dramatic perhaps than flashes of insight, intuition nonetheless often provides solutions to problems when conscious analysis seems fruitless. Since intuition reflects an active, helpful subconscious, it is an asset to a person. Not surprisingly, intuitive people generally differ from non-intuitive people in a number of positive ways: intuitive persons tend to be more self-confident and creative, better able to verbalize thoughts and feelings, less afraid of criticism, and highly individualistic. This is not to say, of course, that intuition is infallible. Neither in his conscious operations nor in his subconscious functioning is man infallible. Still, intuition is a valuable feature in human thought.

The pattern of learning obviously involves storing knowledge in one's memory, that is, in the subconscious mind. As a result much of what we learn becomes automatized. For example, a grown man can speak and walk without giving much conscious attention to the formation of words and steps (5/66, 4). For him (unlike the child who is just learning such actions) these things are automatized, thanks to subconscious programming, and his mind is free to deal with more advanced matters.

We'll now consider still another aspect of subconscious functioning, and one of the most far-reaching: the development and operation of emotions.

13 Emotions

One of the most important functions of the subconscious mind centers on a man's value-judgments.[1]

During his life a man has countless experiences. Some of these give rise to value-judgments: evaluations of various things as being good for him or bad for him. These experiences and value-judgments are filed away in the vast memory bank of his subconscious, and are available for future reference, of a very special kind.

It works like this: Whenever a man confronts some aspect of reality, his subconscious automatically checks that aspect against past experiences and value judgments. Its findings, if any, are then injected into the conscious mind in the form of a unique experience called an emotion.

Notice the exact sequence of events:

1. A man is conscious of some aspect of reality.

2. At lightning speed his subconscious forms an estimate of this aspect of reality. In terms of the man's own values, does this aspect of reality stand in some beneficial or harmful relationship to him? Of what kind? To what degree?

3. This estimate is injected into the conscious mind in the form of a unique experience: an emotion, or feeling, involving the body as well as the mind (it is "psychosomatic").[2]

Since step 2 occurs subconsciously, one is not aware of it;

---

[1] Most of the ideas in this chapter, as well as in the next, are drawn from a series of articles by Nathaniel Branden: "Emotions and Values" (5/66, 1-9); "Emotions and Actions" (6/66, 7-11); "Emotions and Repression" (8/66, 8-16; 9/66, 8-12).

[2] Changes in respiration, muscular tension, and glandular secretion are among the possible bodily consequences of emotions.

to the conscious mind, the sequence of events seems to run from step 1 directly to step 3. Consequently many people are unaware that their emotions are actually value-responses, that emotions are effects of which values are the cause. No emotion is causeless. However, since the crucial evaluation stage, step 2, occurs subconsciously, the cause of a particular emotion can be difficult to trace. We'll say more about this in the next chapter.

Emotions are value-responses, and every value-judgment implies some form of action: recall that a value is that which one *acts* to gain or keep, just as a disvalue is that which one *acts* to shun or destroy. As a result there is another step in the sequence of emotional reaction:

4. Every emotion carries with it an action tendency, a tendency to take some action with regard to the aspect of reality engendering the emotion.

Let's look at some examples[3] in which steps 1, 3, and 4 are identified, step 2 being understood to be a subconscious evaluation.

— A man thinks of his sweetheart (1). He feels love (3), which is the emotional response to that which one values. He is inclined to seek personal, social, or physical contact with her (4).

Several points should be noted in connection with this example.

The man does (or should) consciously know that he values the woman, and he knows why. This is understood in the present discussion. What we are concerned with here is the emotional response only, but we are not suggesting that the emotion exists in an intellectual vacuum. Furthermore, although he feels inclined to seek contact with her, it does not follow that he will or should do so at once. Such action may or may not be appropriate, depending on circumstances. He may be at work, for instance, and must defer being with her until that evening.

— His beloved agrees to become his wife (1). He feels happiness (3), and an urge to celebrate (4).

— Or she declines his proposal (1), and he feels sadness (3) and wants to be alone for a few hours (4).

— A man's car goes out of control (1). He feels fear (3),

---
[3] See also (1/62, 3).

which is the emotional response to that which threatens one's values (such as life). He knows he must act (4) to right the car and avert disaster.

— A criminal tries to harm a man (1). The man feels fear— and hatred (3), the desire to destroy a threat. He is perhaps prompted to kill his enemy (4). (Again, whether or not he should take such action depends on the circumstances. If he can escape and summon the police, killing the criminal would not seem justified.)

These last two examples prompt an important observation: There are no evil emotions. Even fear and the currently much-maligned hatred are perfectly valid emotions. The survival value of such emotions should be obvious. They warn of danger and prompt corrective action: fleeing the danger, righting the situation, or (if necessary) destroying the threatening agent. No emotion is "bad" in itself, and any attempt to wipe out a particular emotion can only lead to frightful sabotaging of one's entire emotional apparatus. Remember: By registering value-estimates—often faster than one can consciously frame an evaluation—emotions can be critically useful to survival. They should not be blamed for problems that actually arise from other factors, such as faulty programming of one's subconscious in the first place. (We'll be discussing emotional problems in the next chapter.)

Although we have treated various emotions as separate experiences, there is also a generalized emotional experience called your *sense of life*. The sense of life is a composite emotion reflecting the general trend of your value-judgments (explicit and implicit), and summing up in one diffuse feeling your basic attitude toward reality. As such it is an ever-present factor in your over-all emotional experience, even if more immediate and intense emotions shift it into the background.

Emotions are a unique kind of experience; you cannot equate an emotion with abstract thought, sense perception, or any other kind of experience. And because emotions are unique, they give life an extra dimension—as well as furnishing real survival benefits. We're very fortunate to have those wonderful things called feelings.

14 Emotional Perplexities

The emotional side of human nature poses some special challenges to the individual.[1] It will help us to understand why if we examine two key facts.

1. In the formation of an emotion, the evaluation stage (listed as step 2 in the last chapter) occurs subconsciously.

This in itself makes the emotional process seem mysterious: a crucial step occurs outside conscious awareness. Hence the first challenge that emotions pose is the temptation to think that emotions just happen without cause or logic. The causes and the logic are there—but are subconscious. No emotion is causeless.

Not only does the emotion seem mysterious; the action tendency accompanying it can be even more puzzling. What should a man do with regard to such an impulse to act? Why, of course, he should examine it rationally so as to determine whether or not the action is justified.

Emotions are not tools of cognition and therefore cannot be tools of decision making. Cognition and decision-making are in the realm of reason, and it is reason that must be the judge of any tentative line of action. Remember that emotions, as value-responses, reflect your estimate of some aspect of reality. That estimate can be mistaken. Your feeling a certain way about some aspect of reality does not prove that your estimate is correct. Consequently your feeling like taking some course of action does not in itself justify your actually doing so. Proof and justification are the job of reason, not emotion.

To put it another way: Reason and emotion are both part of human nature, and each performs its own function. The function

---

[1] See the references given at the beginning of the last chapter.

Emotional Perplexities

of reason is to understand and to guide one's actions accordingly. The function of emotion is to register value-responses. These two functions are clearly not interchangeable.

Just as you cannot expect reason to provide emotional experience, so you cannot expect emotions to serve as guides to action. Such guidance doesn't happen to be the function of emotions. This is why it is courting catastrophe to be guided by emotions and to follow them blindly. To do so is to allow emotions to take the place of reason—a job which they're just not equipped to do.

Incidentally one of the hallmarks of emotional immaturity is to act blindly and automatically on one's impulses. This is the fallacy of the hedonist, who uses pleasure (emotional gratification) as his standard of morality. He has not learned that emotions and their associated action tendencies can be mistaken and must not be followed blindly, and that only a morality of reason can serve his life.

Failure to understand that reason and emotion are not interchangeable leads to another pitfall for the careless individual: the belief that reason and emotion are mutually inimical and contradictory, and that there is therefore a "flaw" in human nature, some sort of rational-emotional dichotomy. After all, it is argued, reason may rule against following a particular emotional impulse; for instance, you may *feel* like killing an enemy, but rationally decide not to. Perfectly true. But what this argument overlooks is that the responsibility of your emotional apparatus ends with the registering of the emotion and action tendency. It is then the job of reason to take over and decide what to do—that is, it is then up to you to focus your mind on the situation and to act according to your rational judgment. The fact that reason can and does overrule emotion hardly can be said to establish any contradiction between them (1/62, 3; 5/66, 6-7).

Of course, the ideal situation would be for reason never to have to overrule emotion, for the emotional action tendency in any given situation always to be correct when measured against rational judgment. But this would require two conditions of the subconscious memory of past experiences and value-judgments.

First, *all* relevant pieces of data that could bear on the situation would have to be present. Obviously this will not always be the case; the situation may contain elements that are new to the man. Second, there would have to be no mistaken judgments bearing on the situation. But no one is infallible. Hence even the most rational of men must expect to encounter situations in which his reason overrules his emotions.

But what of the man who chronically experiences emotional problems? Clearly the data in his subconscious and/or his subconscious functioning are in need of improvement. The most direct way to accomplish such correction would seem to be through examination of his subconscious operations. But this is more easily said than done, and brings us to the second key fact confronting us.

2. It is often difficult or impossible to summon subconscious ideas and operations into the conscious mind.

The conscious mind is slower and of more limited range than the high-speed, vast-memory apparatus of the subconscious, and as a result it can be extremely difficult or even impossible to examine consciously a particular subconscious idea or process.

The ability to focus conscious attention on subconscious thought is part of the art of introspection, and some people are better at it than others. Those most skilled at introspection are persons who, over a period of years (perhaps since childhood), have habitually inquired into the reasons behind their beliefs and feelings. It is only through such constant self-examination that this skill can in time be acquired. A person who has consistently failed to examine his ideas and feelings cannot therefore become proficient at introspection simply by willing it (5/66, 5).

Looking back at the two facts cited above: Because part of the emotional process is subconscious, and because it can be difficult to examine subconscious operations, it follows that a man may encounter difficulty in understanding his own emotions, and therefore in correcting emotional quirks.

The problem is even knottier if a man's value-judgments have not been clearly defined in the first place. The subconscious must then form its value-estimate on the basis of muddy approximations

Emotional Perplexities

filed away in memory where value-judgments should be (5/66, 5).

Then, too, an emotional response may be complex—a mixture of two or more emotions rather than a single one. When this happens, there is the extra difficulty of having to identify the separate emotional components (5/66, 5).

Sometimes a person is only slightly conscious of some aspect of reality, while the subconscious grasps it fully. This results in his feeling an emotion in response to something that he was only barely conscious of, and may have trouble recalling later (5/66, 6).

A more serious problem arises when a man harbors inconsistent value-judgments. Suppose that as a result of past irrationality, two or more contradictory value-judgments are filed away in a man's subconscious. What happens when he is confronted by some aspect of reality bearing upon these judgments? Since the value-judgments are contradictory, the subconscious, with its inexorable logic, will register conflicting emotions accompanied by conflicting action tendencies. A person in such a predicament is beset by two dilemmas: he experiences incompatible emotions, and he experiences impulses to perform contradictory actions—which of course is impossible (6/66, 11).

If a man does have emotional problems, what should he do about them?

Should he simply choose to ignore them and try to live with them? To do so would be immoral. Remember that the standard of morality is life, and that a man's own mental processes are crucially relevant to his life. Hence the deliberate refusal to deal with problems affecting such processes is inimical to life, and therefore wrong.

Equally wrong would be the attempt to nullify troublesome emotions by means of drugs (or excessive indulgence in alcohol). It is the height of savage irrationality to think that if you blind yourself to something it will simply disappear. It won't. Drugs make a problem only seem to melt away. The problem is still present—and probably compounded by the medical effects of the drugs themselves.

Most people understand that physical pain is a warning signal that something is wrong and in need of correction. The same is true of symptoms of emotional problems: they are life-serving signals that some aspect of one's mind is in need of correction.

A man having emotional problems should try to analyze them to discover why a particular aspect of reality engenders a particular feeling. He should probe his own mind in an effort to correct its operations. And if he should fail to make adequate progress with this approach, he should do what he would do if beset by a physical pain whose cause he could not find himself: he should seek professional help.

Symptoms, whether physical or emotional, should not be ignored or masked, for they are important clues that a man can act upon for the purpose of making his life better and happier.

15 Repression

A man programs his own subconscious. Over a period of time many of his conscious mental patterns can become subconsciously automatized. We have seen that this has many beneficial results, such as intuitive and creative insight, the registering of emotions, and the automatization of knowledge.

But if he chooses, a man can also program his subconscious in ways that are harmful to him. It is possible, for instance, to program one's subconscious to block the entry of certain thoughts into consciousness. This is repression.

When a thought is repressed, there is in effect a standing order in the subconscious, an order to block the entrance of the forbidden thought into consciousness.

Why does a man repress a thought? Because he feels threatened by it in some way. It is frightening or painful, and he does not wish to face it.

How does a man repress a thought? By repeatedly evading it and/or expelling it from consciousness. The continual avoidance of the thought finally becomes automatized, that is, the thought has been repressed. Notice that the repression is effected gradually and without the man's even realizing it. The same mechanism that can automatize knowledge and furnish insights has been misused in such a way as to banish a thought from consciousness.

How ironic.

Reason is man's tool of survival; the life-serving effectiveness of reason can only be lessened when it is refused access to a thought—any thought. Repression is a misguided attempt to gain greater control over one's life. But only the opposite effect can result from rendering oneself unable to recall some thought or thoughts (9/66, 11). Hence repression is totally inconsistent with the psychological well-being of a man. It hinders successful living by censoring the thoughts accessible to reason.

Repression frequently involves emotions. Specifically, it is possible to repress awareness of any of the following phases of the emotional process (8/66, 8):

— The aspect of reality whose perception engenders the emotion.
— The kind of emotion experienced.
— The intensity of the emotion.
— The value-judgments underlying the emotion.
— The fact that any emotion is felt at all; a man can tell himself that he feels nothing.

Naturally any of the above forms of emotional repression will interfere with efforts to analyze the emotion(s) involved, and the accompanying action tendency can be so hard to fathom that it's actually frightening.

Since repression is automatized, it cannot be undone by a simple act of the will. In fact, professional therapy is often the only practical approach to the problem of undoing repression. In any event the experiencing of incomprehensible and/or contradictory emotions and action tendencies are common clues that repression is at work (9/66, 12).

A great deal more can be said about repression than we can cover here, and the reader would surely profit from reading Nathaniel Branden's article "Emotions and Repression," cited previously, which describes and gives many examples of this unfortunate practice.

We'll close our discussion of repression with a few observations that can be helpful in avoiding repression.

Although it may be necessary because of circumstances to defer thinking about a particular subject until a later time, a man must avoid relentlessly the temptation to persistently eject from consciousness or evade any thought, whatever it may be, however painful or frightening it may be. Otherwise he runs the risk of repression—and worse, of becoming accustomed to repressing, so that repression itself becomes a characteristic response to thoughts that, for one reason or another, he finds unpleasant (8/66, 15).

Repression

A man should realize that the mere fact of experiencing an emotion is not a moral reflection on him. After all, an emotion is registered automatically, not by choice. Hence, feeling a particular emotion is not relevant to the moral status of a man at the time he feels it.

Failure to realize this is one of the two chief reasons identified by Branden (8/66, 13) as prompting people to repress. The other reason is the false belief that a man must act on an emotion once it is felt. Of course, this is untrue (except perhaps in cases of serious mental illness). But the belief that action will (or, in some sense, should) follow emotions can prompt a man to repress in an effort to avoid ever experiencing an impulse to perform an action which he considers objectionable.

Be prepared to face any thought or feeling, secure in the conviction that you will not act without knowing what you are doing and why. The observance of this advice will go a long way toward the prevention of repression (8/66, 15).

16 Self-Esteem

To live properly, a man must exercise his reason and then act in accordance with it, thereby gaining and keeping values. But reason functions only by choice. Hence we can say that in order to live, a man must choose to live—by choosing to apply himself to the tasks that life requires: thought and value-winning action. The fact that life requires voluntary effort leads to a couple of important implications.[1]

The first implictaion is that a man is not going to make an earnest effort at living unless he believes that he can succeed at it. Nobody makes a serious effort at something he regards as impossible for him. Why knock yourself out if failure is a foregone conclusion? Hence it is vitally important that a man appreciate his own fitness to live. That is, he must realize that he is equipped with an effective survival faculty, which is of course his reason. Your evaluation of your reason, as being an efficacious tool of survival, is your *self-confidence.*

Self-confidence is essential because it is your estimate that you are fit to live, that you are equal to the task of living. A lack of self-confidence is a crippling deficiency because it means you doubt your ability to succeed at living (3/67, 4).

The fact that life requires voluntary effort leads to another important implication, this one having to do with the fact that a man does not act in order to benefit someone unless he values that person. The motivation to help someone falls apart if you do not value him. Now, life requires action. Who is the beneficiary of this

---

[1] The ideas in this chapter are drawn from Nathaniel Branden's series of articles on self-esteem: (3/67, 1-7; 4/67, 5-10; 5/67, 8-11; 6/67, 1-4; 9/67, 8-11).

action? Yourself. It follows that you must value yourself in order to be motivated to act in your own behalf, that is, to apply yourself to the job of living. Your evaluation of yourself as being worth the effort is your *self-respect*.

Self-respect is essential because it provides the motivation to do what has to be done to sustain and forward your life (3/67, 4).

Self-confidence and self-respect are intimately united psychologically. As we saw in chapter 8 they blend to form the composite known as self-esteem.

Self-esteem starts to develop in childhood. In the series of articles cited at the beginning of this chapter, Nathaniel Branden discusses examples of how childhood situations provide the raw material out of which a child shapes—or misshapes—his self-esteem. It is nevertheless possible for an adult to reshape his self-esteem, provided he makes a serious effort at it.

The basis of a healthy self-esteem is rationality: the determination to think, to understand, to conceptualize (3/67, 4-5). A man who fails to make this commitment to reason puts himself in a very tenuous position. Although he may sometimes rely on reason, at other times he permits himself to evade the responsibility of thinking. This means that the over-all pattern of his behavior rests on the premise that it is sometimes beneficial to dispense with reliance on reason. And that premise is strengthened by every irrationally motivated act he performs.

The acceptance, explicit or implicit, of such a premise must logically weaken a man's confidence in his reason (i.e., must weaken his self-confidence). At the same time, his awareness, however peripheral, of his irrationality damages his self-respect. The net effect: irrationality undermines self-esteem.

An unbreached rationality is essential to a healthy self-esteem. From this general principle we can derive some specific guidelines on the development and sustaining of self-esteem.

1. *Do not allow anything to usurp the authority of reason.* Specifically, do not act on any emotion that goes against reason, nor on the opinions of others if such opinions contradict your own judgment. Remember: Every time you betray your reason you are nurturing the cancer of irrationality; the premise that reason can

sometimes be beneficially ignored is strengthened with every breach of rationality.

2. *Strive to maintain sharp mental focus.* The human power of volition is the power to regulate one's consciousness (as we saw in chapter 6). Never use this power to hold your level of awareness below that needed to come to grips with a particular problem. The deliberate avoidance of mental clarity is a technique of evasion.

3. *Have an earnest respect for facts.* Never allow any consideration to take precedence over facts. To do so is a blatant breach of rationality (4/67, 10).

4. *Practice rationality in all areas of your life, not just in your professional work.* Too many people are brilliant and self-assured in their work, while inept and anxiety-ridden when outside their office, laboratory, or classroom (3/67, 7).

5. *Do not be afraid to think.* To submit to such fear is to strengthen it. Be willing to think independently, to act on your own judgment, and to take full responsibility for doing so.

6. *Resist the social pressure to conform.* Don't be intimidated by demands to fit in, by charges of being an oddball or of being divisive (a stock term among those who seek to dominate others), or by challenges like, Who are you to disagree with everyone else? (the cry of an intellectual coward).

7. At the same time *do not make unconventionality for its own sake a value.* If your own rational thought leads you to agree with others, then don't hesitate to do so. There is nothing wrong in going along with a convention provided it seems reasonable to you.

8. *Do not let mistakes shake your self-esteem.* No man is infallible. Strive to avoid mistakes, but don't allow a mistake to weaken your self-esteem.

9. *Never accept an undeserved guilt.* Guilt subdues self-assertiveness (9/67, 9). Much of the vast and ancient assault on self-esteem is carried on by those who traffic in guilt. They preach that it is sinful to be prosperous, sinful to be proud, sinful to be capable of enjoying sexual fulfillment, sinful to *be* (i.e., they preach the obscenity of "original sin"). Examine very critically any allegation imputing guilt; you will most likely discover that it is

a lie. If on the other hand you do commit an action which *you* regard as immoral, then you have to face and accept the corresponding guilt. Don't evade, rationalize, or repress it, but don't be overwhelmed by it either. Resolve not to let such a thing happen again, and then get on with the job of living.

10. *Seek constantly to expand your knowledge, understanding, and abilities.* It is in this way that self-esteem is maintained (6/67, 2). Never succumb to the idea that you've thought enough. Be intellectually active, learning new things, acquiring new skills and sharpening old ones. To a human being, for whom reason is the key to life, intellectual stagnation is spiritual death.

Self-esteem is crucial to life. The need for self-esteem is so great that a man who is deficient in it seeks to fake it—an attempt at which the wretch inevitably fails. Nothing can take the place of true self-esteem; reality is not a thing to be cheated.

In striving for self-esteem, as in all areas of life, a good rule is: Accept no substitutes.

17 A Summary and a Preview

We are approaching the end of our discussion of man as an individual. In the next chapter we begin a discussion of man as a social being. The principles we'll derive in upcoming chapters, which deal with society, will depend on those derived in previous chapters, which dealt with the individual. The reason for this should be obvious. Society is, after all, a collection of individuals. Guidelines for society must be based upon the nature of the units of which society is composed, that is, individual human beings. It is logically invalid to theorize about society as if it were some sort of primary, irreducible to any constitutive units. The usual result of such theorizing is the theorist's insistence that men change from what they are into beings more in keeping with the theorist's wishes. Our investigation of society will follow from our discussion of the individual. Any other approach is a waste of time.

Here is a summary of the major points covered in previous chapters:

* Man, as a living organism, faces the alternatives of life and death.

* Our senses are our channels of information from the outside world. They are reliable, although we must learn to interpret sense data. It is most inadvisable to tamper with sensory operation.

* But our senses are only the starting point of our knowledge. Reason is man's formal tool of cognition—and survival. It is by means of reason that a man thinks, understands, conceptualizes, expands his knowledge through logic, and forwards his life.

* Reason functions only by choice. Man has the power to adjust his level of rational awareness. This is his free will. Man is a being of volitional consciousness.

* Life requires the acquisition, retention, use, and enjoyment of values.

A Summary and a Preview

* Values must be arranged in a hierarchy, since it is often necessary to choose between values. The supreme values are reason (which is man's tool of survival), purpose (which organizes his life), and self-esteem (which provides his sense of competence and worthiness to live).

* A code of values accepted by choice is a code of morality. The moral (good) is the rational and life-serving. The immoral (evil) is the irrational and life-negating.

* Man has a duality of awareness: perceptual and conceptual. Because of the ease and directness of perception, man experiences a desire for concretization of his concepts. This tendency accounts for various forms of human behavior.

* There is a subconscious side to the human mind. The subconscious is a vast-memory, high-speed computer which assists man in many ways.

* Emotions are subconsciously triggered value-responses. They are very useful, although if misunderstood, they can be a source of difficulty.

* Man has a basic need for self-esteem, for a sense of his own fitness and worthiness to live.

We have also described some of the ways in which a man can subvert his mind (and therefore hinder his life):

* Tampering with his senses, say through the use of drugs.

* Evasion: the deliberate refusal to focus his mind on some thought.

* Holding contradictory values, or failing to hierarchically organize his values.

* Lack of purpose.

* Faulty concepts of morality.

* Mistaken ideas about the origin of emotions.

* Acting blindly on emotions instead of acting solely on reason.

* Repression of various kinds.

* Various practices inimical to self-esteem (see previous chapter).

A great many of these points deal with human psychology. This is because no discussion of man and his life can ignore psychology. In order for a man to live the life of a man, he has to be aware of, evaluate, and regulate his mental processes; in other words, he must understand the basics of psychology.

I stress, however, that I am not a professional psychologist and that the treatment of psychology given here deals with the fundamentals relevant to successful living and is not offered as exhaustive. Nor should anyone afflicted with serious psychological problems regard any book as a substitute for professional therapy.

What has been the viewpoint from which this book's psychological concepts have been developed? From the viewpoint of the book as a whole: life. Our ideas in psychology (like those in philosophy and morality) have revolved around the requirements for successful human living. Nathaniel Branden, who published the foundation papers in this field, has designated it *biocentric psychology*.

The quality of mental functioning advocated in this book is that which characterizes the state of mental health. When a man's body is functioning appropriately for his survival, we say that he is physically healthy. Likewise, when his mind is functioning in a way conducive to his survival, he is mentally healthy.

PART THREE

18 Knowledge and Progress

An individual human being is a complete entity in himself.[1] A man alone on a desert island could survive (provided the island's resources were sufficient for his needs). Yet few people would choose such a way of life. Virtually anyone, given the opportunity to live an isloated existence, would prefer to remain a member of *society*—that mode of living in which individuals interact with one another in various ways.

Evidently people regard living in a society as a value. Why?

A rational man defines something as a value only if he considers it necessary or useful to his life. Hence he can regard living in a society as a value only if he believes that such a way of life benefits him in some way.

Were it not for the benefit they derive from living in a society, individuals would not have created society in the first place. Hence we can say that *the sole purpose and justification of society is its usefulness to its individual members.*

What other purpose and justification could there be?

Just what are the advantages that the individual can derive from living in a society? One of the most important has to do with knowledge.

Man is part of the vast universe. In order to live, he must acquire knowledge about the universe, and apply that knowledge to his life. As we have seen, he can do these things only by vol-

---

[1] Except with regard to biological reproduction.

untarily exercising his rational faculty. But consider the advantage of living in a society: rather than having to try to discover as much knowledge as he can on his own, he has in a society the opportunity to learn from others. Each generation can have available to it the knowledge acquired by past generations, instead of having to start from the beginning. The individual is thereby relieved of the burden of having to rediscover things that have already been discovered; he can be taught these things instead, and this allows him to acquire maximum knowledge in minimum time.

This leads to other advantages. For one thing, by being relieved of the task of trying to rediscover the old, a man has the opportunity to discover the new. He can use the knowledge he has been taught as a base from which to build, thereby possibly discovering new knowledge, which he can elect to pass on to his contemporaries and to future generations. In this way accumulated knowledge expands, and the members of society are the richer for it.

Furthermore, he has the opportunity to devise new applications for existing knowledge. The acquisition of knowledge for its own sake is a value because such learning keeps the mind active and nourishes self-esteem, but the chief value of knowledge lies in its application to the problems of life. A man's opportunity for inventiveness is maximized when he is relieved of having to acquire all his knowledge through his own trial and error. As with new discoveries, a man may elect to pass on the fruits of his inventiveness to others, thereby enriching their lives.

Such inventiveness often takes the form of what we appropriately call inventions—devices and processes that make life better. A machine, being the product of human inventiveness, is a crystallization of thought. It is a material embodiment of intellectual knowledge, knowledge of the laws of nature on which the machine is based. A machine is built out of inanimate matter, but the choice of materials, the way in which these materials are formed into parts, and the plan by which the parts are united to form the whole—these are all products of human intelligence and rational thought. Consequently machines are reflections of the highest human qualities—no less than are symphonies and paintings. Remember this the next time you encounter someone who is afraid of machines, or who regards these products of human thought as "dehumanizing" influences. The fact that irrational men can use machines for evil purposes does not negate the fact that the creation of a machine requires the most deeply human of all activities: purposeful thought.

We have seen that living in a society greatly increases a man's opportunity to discover and invent. If the discoverer or inventor chooses to share the results of his efforts with others, he thereby enriches their lives. This is a principal form of what we call human progress. Bear in mind, however, that such progress is the achievement of creative *individuals*. Society neither discovers nor invents anything; individuals do. I stress this because there is a tendency nowadays to ignore the individual as the cause of human progress, and to consider society as the source (in some mystical way) of human betterment.

Of course, men may choose to cooperate in trying to solve a particular problem. This involves their communicating their thoughts to one another in the hope that some man present will eventually be able to arrive at a solution from these pooled ideas. Nevertheless, thought remains an activity that can occur only within an individual human mind. There is no such thing as a collective brain or collective thinking.

Progress is not an inevitable concomitant of society. It is an indirect effect, which depends on individuals to generate it. Hence, even with regard to progress the justification of society still lies in its usefulness to its individual members, some of whom may be able and willing, as a secondary consequence, to enrich the lives of the rest of us.

19 Production and Trade

The communication of knowledge is important to man. But so are many material things. As a biological organism a man requires food—as well as clothing and shelter to protect him from the elements. These material goods have to be *produced*—made from raw materials by purposeful human effort.

Living in isolation, a man would have to try to produce all these things for himself. But living in a society offers him a tremendous advantage: rather than having to try to produce all these things for himself, he has the opportunity in a society to specialize in his productive efforts so that he can then *trade* with others. In the simplest workable situation, trade would be by barter; the man who produced bread would produce more than he personally needed and then trade the surplus to other men for their respective products, like shoes or fuel. A more efficient approach is to use a medium of exchange—money—to accomplish trade.

Note that money is a consequence of production and a tool of trade. Since production and trade greatly improve the lives of men, it is absurd to imagine that "money is the root of all evil"—unless one equates life with evil (as those who mouth this slogan implicitly do). The life-serving is the good, and money is instrumental in improving life (through trade). Hence we may say that money is in fact the root of much good. For a superb discussion of this topic, read Francisco's comments on the nature and meaning of money in Miss Rand's *Atlas Shrugged* (Part II, chap. 2).

There are some important observations to be made about production in a specifically industrial society such as ours. These have to do with what has been called the Pyramid of Ability.

The ability referred to here is that of understanding various

Production and Trade

phases of reality, such as the laws of nature, and applying such knowledge to the problems of producing goods. In short, we mean *productive* ability.

Experience shows that men differ in ability, and this is one of the outstanding facts of life in a society. Men differ in native intelligence, acquired aptitudes, and developed talents. Consequently they form a hierarchy or pyramid of ability, and this is especially relevant in an industrial society, as we shall now see.

We begin by considering a man living in isolation, on a desert island. A man in such a situation will have to exert a great deal of mental and physical effort in order to achieve but a modicum of benefit. He may, for instance, have to spend a whole day hunting in order to obtain the meat of some small animal. Or it may take him days of exhausting effort to build a makeshift shelter. If we compare the rewards of his efforts with the labor that goes into achieving them, we find that through very hard work he achieves only a bare-subsistence standard of living.

Now, consider the position of that same man in a society such as ours. Suppose he finds work operating a machine in a factory, pushing buttons or pulling levers. Clearly, the effort required by this job is far less than he would have had to exert in order to survive on the desert island. On the other hand, he enjoys a far better standard of living than he could have attained living in isolation. In other words, as a factory worker, he works less but lives better than he could have as a hermit.

The amount of labor demanded by his job is fairly modest and yet wins him a good standard of living in a society like ours. This same amount of effort would bring him virtually no benefit on the desert island.

What accounts for the difference?

What acounts for the fact that a mild expenditure of mental and physical effort, that would not even suffice to insure his bare survival were he isolated, can enable him to live in comfort in modern America? Why is his employer willing to pay him a good wage for performing the relatively mild mental and physical activity involved in pushing buttons? Evidently it is because the machine which this man is operating plays a part in the manufacturing of the product marketed by the company. As a result the operating of this machine is of sufficient importance to the employer to motivitate him to pay a man to perform this task.

It boils down to this: The amount of labor being discussed here has in itself very little life-serving potential for a man, being only a fraction of the effort needed to effect his survival were he isolated. But this same amount of effort rises sharply in life-serving potential when applied to the operation of a machine at the behest of an employer in an industrial society.

Now, consider this: The man operating the machine did not design it or build it. Very likely he wouldn't have known how to create the machine he's operating. Moreover, he didn't conceive and develop the product which the machine is helping to make, the product whose manufacture is the reason his employer retains him at all. Other men, with greater ability than he has exhibited, created the product and the means for producing it. It is *their* achievement that accounts for the surplus value of his labor. *They* are responsible for the fact that his labor brings him the reward it does instead of what such effort would bring him in a situation devoid of such men. Their accomplishments are what infuse meaning and value into what would otherwise be pointless activity on his part.[1]

If you doubt the validity of what is being said here, try the following experiment:

1. Obtain a large cardboard box, and fit it with push-buttons, levers, or other such devices.

2. Stand before it for an hour or so, pushing the buttons and operating the levers in some sequence of your own choosing.

3. When you are done, figure out in what way and to what extent you have improved your life through the activity of step 2.

What's that you say? You haven't profited at all from this labor? And yet in a factory the same effort could earn you a

---

[1] It may be objected that a man working even as an unskilled laborer might have unrealized ability. Quite true. But in the present discussion we are concerned with the actual rather than the potential, since it is the actual that produces results. A man owes it to himself to exhibit and develop his full ability.

living. But in a factory you would be following instructions that other men have given you about the operating of a machine that other men have devised to make a product that other men have created. It would be due to the contributions of all these abler others that *you* could earn a living through such moderate effort. Thus you would be benefiting from the ability of abler men (including those who brought about the many products you buy with the money you earn).

But, you may object, without the efforts of the labor force, the product would never be made at all, and the company would go out of business; and this proves that the blue-collar workers are vital to the entire production enterprise. Absolutely correct. A careful reading of the foregoing discussion will show that this fact, far from being disputed, is central to what has been said. Our machine operator and his fellow workers *are* important; that's why they are paid to do what they do. The question being considered here is: *What* accounts for the importance of what they do? Certainly not the kind or degree of effort they expend. Rather, it is that this effort is in the service of a productive enterprise generated by the staff in laboratory and office. No attempt is being made to downgrade these workers; rather, we are identifying the *source* of the value which their labor admittedly has.

At first sight it may seem that this whole argument is reversible. Since, as we have affirmed, the labor of the machine operator is vital to the solvency of the company, don't the engineers and executives benefit from *his* labor? Yes, from his labor. But not from his ability; they already possess that much ability themselves. Follow this closely. A useful test for comparing the degrees of ability required to do two different jobs is this: (1) Assume that Jones has just enough ability to perform job A, while Smith has just enough ability to perform job B. (2) Now, ask yourself which man would have greater difficulty in learning the job of the other. That man's present job is the one requiring less ability. Example: a physician versus a janitor.[2]

---

[2] Sometimes the result is a toss-up. Example: a physician vs. an astrophysicist.

Suppose, now, that Jones's job is to create or market products, while Smith's is to operate a machine. Which man exhibits greater ability? Can it seriously be argued that Jones benefits from Smith's *ability?* After all, Jones could easily learn Smith's job. Can the opposite statement be made? But as we have seen, Smith does indeed benefit from Jones's ability, which creates the value that Smith's labor has. Clearly it is the machine operator who profits from the ability of the executive and engineer, not the other way around.

The engineer and the machine operator need each other's labor; to that extent, they are even up. But in terms of productive ability, the benefits flow unilaterally, from engineer to machine operator. The engineer could easily learn to operate the machine. He does not do so because his surplus ability would then be wasted. The machine operator, on the other hand, would exhibit a deficit of ability were he to try to do the job of an engineer.

It may be asked, Don't the engineers and executives benefit from the ability of others? Yes: from those *above* them in the pyramid, such as the scientists who formulated the laws and principles drawn upon in engineering.

And so it goes. Each man benefits from the achievements of those whose ability exceeds his.

There is good reason for our stressing these facts. Industrialists, corporate executives, and professionals are often regarded as "exploiters," while the men in the shop are considered to be the true producers. The men at the top are begrudged their handsome salaries as being grabbed at the expense of the workers' sweat. Our purpose here is to set the record straight, as it should have been set a hundred years ago. Although the efforts of all employees are needed, the benefits of ability flow one way, the only way they can: from the more able to the less.

To be specific: Thomas Edison benefited mankind by inventing things that made life better for all men—few of whom could have equaled his achievements. But moreover, he created the base of a whole new set of industries, and thereby brought about a market for the services of men to work in these industries. All these workers, then and now, owe thanks for most of their income to men like Edison, men whose achievements give importance—and therefore value—to the labor that earns those incomes, labor that would not suffice to earn a single day's food for men living in a situation in which there were no Edisons.

The time has come to stop begrudging the men at the top their financial rewards; they earn them. They also deserve the good will and gratitude of the rest of us.

It's about time we paid up.

20 Visibility

In chapter 10 we considered the perceptual-conceptual duality in human consciousness. We found that a man tends to value objects of perception which concretize his conceptual knowledge and thereby enable him to apprehend such abstract knowledge with the ease and directness of perception. We turn our attention now to a deeply important kind of concretization, one having to do with life in a society.[1]

During the course of his life a person grows in many ways. Not only does he undergo bodily development; as a conscious entity he undergoes psychological development, building an amazingly complex structure of thoughts, values, attitudes, and feelings. This galaxy of psychological traits and characteristics constitutes his psychological self (which we'll refer to as his self for brevity). Several observations should now be made about the self.

First of all, since man is a being of volitional consciousness, his self is largely of his own making; he has created it.

Second, a man's self is of crucial importance to him, being the sum of all the things that form his psychological identity. Hence his self is an ever-present factor in his behavior.

Third, a man is aware of his self conceptually; it is not an object he can grasp by perception. We'll refer to a man's concept of his self as his self-image.

Finally, because of the concretization tendency (discussed in chapter 10), a man will tend to value anything that has the power to concretize or objectify his self-image. Because this concept is so crucial to him, he will value very highly whatever can enable him to grasp this concept in the manner of perception.

---

[1] The material in this chapter, as well as in the next, is drawn from Nathaniel Branden's article "Self-Esteem and Romantic Love" (12/67, 1-8; 1/68, 1-7; 2/68, 1-5).

Visibility

But how can this concretization be achieved? A man can perceive his physical face in a mirror; what mirror can allow him to perceive his psychological face, his self-image?

Any such mirror must be capable of reflecting the intricacies of a human consciousness. The only thing that can match the richness and many-sidedness of a human consciousness is: *another* human consciousness.

Branden refers to this experience as "visibility."

How exactly is this experience of visibility achieved in practice? Through a feedback process: when you interact with another person, he responds to you, and your perception of his response can lead to your experiencing visibility. The process can be outlined as follows:

1. YOUR SELF. This is the starting point.
2. YOUR ACTIONS. These follow from your self.
3. THE OTHER PERSON'S SELF. These determine the evaluation he forms of you from your actions.
4. HIS ACTIONS IN RESPONSE TO YOU. These follow from his evaluation of you.
5. YOUR EVALUATION OF HIS ACTIONS. This involves your estimate of how well his actions in response to you compare with your own self-image. To the extent that his actions toward you correspond to your self-image, you experience visibility. To the extent that his actions toward you clash with your self-image, you do not experience visibility.

Each of these steps influences the degree of visibility experienced. Let's examine them more closely.

1. Your self, as the source of your actions, is what generates the process.

2. Other people cannot look directly into your mind. They can know you only by your actions: what you say and do, and how you say and do it. Ideally your actions are expressions of your *true* self.

Any discrepancy between your self and your actions will hamper visibility because the behavior which others perceive and react to will reflect the fictitious self you are projecting rather than your true self.

Such discrepancy can arise in different ways. One example is role-playing—assuming different personalities in different encounters (12/67, 7). This practice can easily become automatized; beware of it. Excessive aloofness should also be avoided, as should, of course, deliberate misrepresentation. Being yourself is the only rational approach to social interaction.

3. Once the other person perceives you through your actions, what determines how he will respond to you? Obviously, his own psychological characteristics—especially his values—are the yardstick by which he will gauge you. Suppose, for instance, that your actions reflect the virtue of rationality. Another person's response to you will certainly be influenced by his view of rationality. Does he regard it as a noble human quality, or as narrow-mindedness or heartlessness?

Another person's response to you does not depend solely on your actions; it depends jointly on (*a*) your actions and (*b*) his evaluation of them.

This is what accounts for your eliciting different responses from different people, for your not feeling equally close to all the people you know. It depends on how well their values correlate with yours, on the degree of mutuality of mind and values, which Branden calls *spiritual affinity* (1/68, 5).

Where spiritual affinity is high (and there are no other factors hampering visibility), the other person will be a friend: he will react to you as you would react to yourself in the person of another (12/67, 5). The result: gratifying visibility.

Where there is little spiritual affinity, although no actual clash of mind and values, he will seem distant and uninteresting.

Where his values actually contradict your own, there will be a clash of personalities. He will seem hostile to some degree, and you will feel misunderstood (12/67, 7).

It is especially important to understand this last case. If the other person's values clash with yours, then he will respond negatively to the very qualities you take pride in having. It will be not your faults he holds against you but your virtues (virtues by your code, but not by his). A moment's thought will show that this is the only reaction logically possible to him in a situation in which his values contradict yours.

Therefore, if someone seems hostile for no apparent reason, do not be too quick to assume the blame. It may well be that he has been offended by qualities about you which *you* regard as desirable. So, don't blame yourself. To do is to blame your moral code, your value code, and to assume implicitly that his code is superior to yours. You thereby betray your own reason, which is the source of your code, and accept in its place the ideas of another person, thereby conceding his moral superiority over you and granting that his mind is somehow better than yours. Such an assumption is a breach of reason and honor. It can lead to the evil practice of trying to win him over by role-playing, by acting in a manner which seems likely to win his approval. But it stands to reason that by betraying your own code you will not win him over but will rather surrender yourself over to him. If you really believe in your own code, your attitude will be, "Take me for what I am, or not at all."

Of course, this does not mean that a person should walk around with a chip on his shoulder. Only the immature go out of their way to offend others. A truly rational man neither desires nor needs interpersonal friction to bolster his self-esteem, and tries to get along with other people as harmoniously as honor will permit.

4. Ideally the other person's attitude toward you will be reflected in his actions. In fact, however, there may be a discrepancy between his evaluation of you and his actions toward you. He may indulge in role-playing, through habit or deliberate insincerity. Or he may simply not be very demonstrative. Some people tend to camouflage their true feelings, say with humor.

Of course, a rational man will generally prefer people who are frank and open. Nevertheless, he should not overlook the fact that interpreting the responses of others is an art worth developing.

5. The degree of visibility you achieve depends upon how well the feedback you receive from others tallies with your own self-image. It follows that you must have a self-image in the first place.

One of the most tragic of vices is to attempt to achieve one's self-image through interaction with others. Since, as we have seen, different people will respond to you differently, any attempt to form a self-image from these varied, and often inconsistent, responses is doomed to failure. Besides, such an attempt is wholly illogical, since it attempts to create the cause out of what should be the effect.

It is also important that man's self-image be fairly accurate. A woman of sixty will be disappointed with her reflection in a mirror if she fancies herself as having the youthful beauty of a girl of nineteen. Likewise, the more illusions a man has about his true self, the more disappointing and frustrating will be his search for visibility, since whatever accurate feedback he does receive will fail to square off with his inaccurate self-image.

Another impediment to visibility is repression. Repressed material is blocked from consciousness. To the extent that a man represses, to that extent he is unknown to himself, and his self-image is incomplete. It follows that any visibility he experiences will be less than ideal (12/67, 8).

Production, trade, progress, and the communication of knowledge—these are the previously discussed advantages possible to an individual in a society. But the Visibility Principle names another benefit, one of profound personal significance to a man: the possibility of achieving visibility—self objectification—through interaction with others. The value of visibility should not be overlooked or sold short by anyone, even the most rational and rugged individualist. To do so is to defy a fact of human nature: the deep value of self-objectification, a value stemming from the perceptual-conceptual duality of awareness and the nature of the self-image.

We have seen that greater visibility is possible when the feedback received from others tallies well with one's self-image; the better the correlation between feedback and self-image, the richer the visibility experience. Some people you meet will respond more fully to your psychological self than will others. Specifically, there is one tremendously important aspect of your self that only about half the people you meet can personally respond to: your sexuality. Only persons of the opposite sex have the potential to offer you full visibility, a potential realized in a romantic-sexual relationship—our next topic of discussion.

21 Sexuality

Human sexuality involves much more than the mere biological fact of being either male or female. Psychologically, you are aware of your own sexuality, and you develop many attitudes on sexual matters such as: sex in general, the opposite sex, your own body, the body of the opposite sex, the respective sexual roles of men and women, your own sexual role (1/68, 1-2). In other words, part of your self is determined by your awareness of your sexuality and by the attitudes and premises you have adopted about sex.

For the fullest experience of visibility, the sexual aspect of your self must be responded to by the other person.

Only a member of the opposite sex can respond to your sexuality. For example, a woman views a man from a perspective impossible to another (normal) man: she views him as a being of contrasting sexuality. His maleness is something special from her viewpoint, and this adds a dimension to her total response to him. (Another man's response to him lacks this dimension.) Similarly a man can respond more fully to a woman than can another woman.

In general, then, the visibility experienced with a member of the opposite sex is enhanced over that experienced with a member of one's own sex, other things being equal. This is true in any man-woman relationship, whether casual or deep. One never deals with any member of the opposite sex in a manner completely oblivious of his or her contrasting sexuality. So-called Platonic relationships are not to be found in real life, at least not among healthy people.

This is not to say that a rational person seeks to take to bed every member of the opposite sex encountered. There is a whole spectrum of relationships possible between any two people. The relationship between a man and a woman can range from casual acquaintanceship to the deepest relationship of all: the romantic-sexual relationship.

The word "romantic" implies love, while a "sexual" relationship brings to mind the intense pleasure of sexual intercourse. We now trace the development of the romantic-sexual relationship from the concepts of (1) love, and (2) pleasure.

1. Love is your emotional response to that which you value. If you love a person, it is because that person embodies your highest values. In other words, a high spiritual affinity is essential for a true love relationship.

2. Pleasure plays a cardinal role in human life. It is not a luxury but a necessity. Pleasure is the natural reward for life-serving action, and an incentive to persist in such action. Because pleasure is the consequence of efficacious action, it conveys a sense of being "in control" of one's life. *It is through pleasure that one experiences his own efficacy.*[1]

Any love relationship, even between members of the same sex, entails a certain amount of pleasure. The high spiritual affinity affords rich visibility, and the persons involved derive much pleasure from being together, talking together, and sharing various experiences. And since this pleasure is the consequence of visibility, it is a payment one receives for being the kind of person he is. When you are with someone you love and who loves you—loves you for the right reasons, for the things for which you want to be loved—the consequent pleasure is a form in which you celebrate in honor of yourself, in honor of the person you have chosen to be and who is made visible to you in the relationship. At the same time, your pleasure is your tribute to your friend, a tribute for his being what he is: the personification of the things you value. Such is the beauty of love and friendship.

Since part of your self is your sexual identity, to which only a member of the opposite sex can fully respond, it is with a member of the opposite sex that a love relationship can be the most

---

[1] See "The Psychology of Pleasure" by Nathaniel Branden (2/64, 5-6).

rewarding. In a romantic relationship your beloved reflects your deepest image of yourself, affording the richest of visibility and preparing the way for a sexual relationship.

Sexual pleasure is of course intense. But more importantly, it is integrated: it is a pleasure of both mind and body. While some pleasures are chiefly intellectual (like reading a good book) and others are chiefly physical (like enjoying fine food), sex is a pleasure of the whole person. Remember that your psychological self is crucially entwined in your sex life. The kind of person you are determines your sexual attitudes—and your choice of a partner.

You choose a sexual partner with whom you enjoy a high spiritual affinity, a high mutuality of mind and values. This is the crucial non-physical aspect of sex; were it not for this, any partner would do, just as any male dog suffices for a bitch in heat. If you are tempted to regard sex as a purely bodily pleasure, ask yourself why *whom* you sleep with matters to you. What accounts for your having many acquaintances of the opposite sex whom you would not choose as sexual partners, even though they probably are physically compatible with you? Isn't it because they are not spiritually compatible? A moment's reflection will show that your partner's personality, which reflects his or her mind and values, is deeply important to you. Hence sex is a pleasure not just of the body but of body and mind—an integrated pleasure. (1/68, 4.)

All the previously mentioned benefits of love apply in the extreme to sexual love. Since pleasure in general is a form of experiencing your own efficacy, and since sexual pleasure in particular is integrated, sexual pleasure affirms that your life is a value and that you are efficacious in living (i.e., it affirms your self-esteem). In sex you experience being an end in yourself (1/68, 5). At the same time, you pay the highest of tributes to your partner by affirming that he or she personifies your highest values and is desired by you on that basis, the basis of the kind of person he or she has chosen to be.

One implication from all this is that sex should not be treated lightly. Those who indulge in sexual escapades fail to realize that sex is simply too important to be exercised recklessly.

Some such people undoubtedly try to use sex to achieve the

self-esteem of which sex is a celebration. Going through the motions of a celebration will not create something to celebrate; that must come first. The effect cannot create the cause. Hence a sexual relationship indulged in to compensate for spiritual emptiness can only have frustration as its consequence.

Because sex is an act of self-celebration, it is despised by those enemies of humanity who seek to humble and degrade man. The tactics have taken many forms.

— For centuries sex was denounced as sinful. This was done as a means of trying to degrade man, and was very effective for two reasons. First, sex is a natural capacity. If a man could be convinced that sex is sinful, then he could only conclude logically that he was (at least partially) evil by nature. Second, the rational exercise of sex is a form of self-celebration. Convincing a man that such celebration is sinful could go a long way toward undermining his self-esteem. For these reasons to attack sex was one of the most terrible and effective weapons in the war on man waged by those who had ceased to be men themselves.

— It is often claimed even today that sex before marriage is sinful. A man and woman marry when each has decided that the other is a permanent choice for a partner in life. Clearly such a final choice goes beyond the requirements for a sensible sexual relationship.

One chooses and is chosen by a sexual partner for reason of spiritual affinity, as we have seen. Such a choice is not necessarily final—or exclusive. As long as a sexual relationship is mutually voluntary and based on values, it is proper. If a man and woman decide to choose each other permanently and exclusively, then they can finalize their relationship by marrying. After that each has the right to exclusive sexual enjoyment of the other, this being one of the understandings upon which marriage is based. (For this reason extramarital sex is wrong; it is a fraud against the faithful partner by violating the condition of exclusivity.)

— It is still shouted from the pulpits of the world that the primary (if not sole) purpose of sex is procreation. To understand the viciousness of this claim, consider that the spiritual aspect of human sexuality, the mutuality of mind and values, is what distinguishes the sexuality of man from that of animals; the reproductive aspect, on the other hand, is one that man shares with animals. Could it be that those who attack the non-reproductive aspect of human sexuality, the distinctively human aspect, are seeking to obscure in the minds of men the difference between a man and an animal? Judge for yourself.

Let us be quite plain: there is nothing especially human or moral about impregnation, gestation, and birth; alley cats can accomplish as much. The distinctively human aspect of sex is spiritual, not biological.

Let me hasten to add that there are specifically human aspects of reproduction. However, these have to do with rationally *planning* a family so that the children are genuinely wanted and are provided for properly and lovingly. In any event the procreative aspect of human sexuality is secondary and optional, to be made use of by married persons who choose freely to do so. (Only married persons are in a position to offer a stable home life since they have chosen each other irrevocably—it is to be hoped.)

One special form of this particular attack on human sexuality is the attack on contraception. The denunciation of birth control is nothing less than a denunciation of the enjoyment of sex as a means of self-celebration. It is a claim that a man and woman cannot persistently enjoy sex for their own sakes, but only for the sake of children yet to be born. It is a misanthropic attempt to attach strings to the achievement of joy through sex. For an excellent analysis of this tactic see Ayn Rand's article "Of Living Death" (9/68, 1-6; 10/68, 1-6; 11/68, 1-4).

Sex is of profound importance to each of us. For a rational person it can be a source of immense joy. For others it can reap shame, guilt, suffering. Involved as sex is with one's whole self, it should not be surprising that psychological disorders often involve sexual symptoms. But one thing is certain: whatever sex brings a person, whether joy or misery, it is a consequence of the kind of person he has made himself. In sex one gets what one has earned—one way or the other.

22 The Nature of Freedom

So far we have considered only the advantages that an individual can derive from living in a society. We have yet to discuss the risks that society presents to him. An understanding of what these risks are (and of what can be done about them) rests upon first understanding the concept of human freedom, and we now turn our attention to this concept.

What is freedom? One answer that might be offered is, "Freedom is the absence of restraints on an individual's actions." Many people would probably accept this as a definition of freedom. But as we shall see, this description of freedom is far from satisfactory.

No definition is sound if it ignores the facts of reality. For instance, were we to define a scientist as "one who is incapable of making a mistake," we would be ignoring the fact of human fallibility. As a result our definition would be unrealistic, and therefore useless. Moreover, such a definition would imply that scientists don't exist, for if one accepts the fact of human fallibility, then it logically follows that any allegedly infallible men must be non-existent. Hence the above definition would relegate scientists to the class of impossibilities, along with square circles and perpetual-motion machines. Of course, few people would accept such a definition of a scientist in the first place. But note that anyone who did would have to conclude that the very concept of "scientists" is useless by reason of impossibility. Such are the fruits of an unreasonable definition.

The same problem arises if freedom is defined as being simply "the absence of restraints on an individual's actions." Such a definition ignores the fact that the laws of nature impose certain limitations on man and thereby make the absence of any and all restraints impossible. For example, a man cannot live without thought, survive for long without food, fly under his own muscle power, or practice clairvoyance. To define freedom simply as the absence of restraints is to ignore these facts and to thereby make freedom seem an impossibility. Obviously, if to be free a man must be able to defy the facts of reality, then freedom is an illusion.

Few people would accept a definition which implied that scientists don't exist. Unfortunately far too many people accept an unsound definition of freedom, one that leads them to conclude that freedom is impossible. One reason that such misunderstanding is so wide-spread is that those who are less than enthusiastic about freedom promote confusion and fallacy with such arguments as, "Freedom is an illusion; man can never be free from his needs, his natural limitations, his dependence on nature, etc., etc." To avoid being misled by such arguments, and to truly understand freedom, one must arrive at a realistic definition of the concept, a definition that takes cognizance of the facts of reality instead of ignoring them. Such a definition follows:

Full freedom is the absence of restraints, other than natural ones, on an individual's actions.

By acknowledging the existence of natural limitations on human activity, our definition is realistic and identifies freedom as being in the realm of the possible. The reason for including the adjective "full" is that freedom can exist in different degrees—a point we're about to examine more closely—and hence our first step had to be to identify the maximum possible degree of freedom, which we have designated full freedom.

What influences can make a man's freedom less than full? Since we do not regard natural limitations as being in any way relevant to a man's degree of freedom, it follows that only restraints which are not natural in origin can reduce a man's degree of freedom.

The degree of a man's freedom decreases as the restraints on his actions, beyond those imposed by nature, increase in number or extent.

The question now arises, What, aside from the laws of nature, can restrict a person's actions, thereby reducing his freedom? The answer is not hard to find. Alone on a desert island, a man would enjoy full freedom. Nothing would limit his activity except the laws of nature.[1] Clearly, then, freedom-reducing influences can arise only in a social context, which means that they arise in some way from other people. A moment's reflection leads to the following conclusion:

Although the influences reducing a man's freedom can vary in form, the source of any and all such influences can only be the actions of other men.

We shall designate such influences "social" restraints, to distinguish them from natural ones. It is, of course, necessary to distinguish between natural and social restraints because the difference between them is overwhelming. Natural restraints are facts of reality, absolutes about whose existence man has no say, while social restraints (such as human laws, for example) are plastic and are shaped and reshaped by human action.

The forms of social restraints on individual action range from objective legal regulations to mob violence. But note that regardless of the form, any such freedom-reducing influence necessarily arises, in one way or another, from the actions of others.

I do not suggest that all forms of social restraint are essentially evil. In fact, we shall see that certain social restraints are reasonable and justified. Our purpose in this chapter has been to define and objectively describe the nature of human freedom, to demonstrate that freedom is not impossible or illusory, to show that freedom can exist in different degrees, and to identify the variables that affect one's degree of freedom as social restraints rather than natural ones. The next points to consider are the value of freedom to a man and the proper kind of freedom for an individual in a social context.

---

[1] Even if he contracted a disease, this would merely be a result of the biological fact that a man can be incapacitated by a microbe. Such incapacitation would place additional restrictions on his activity, but these restrictions would still be natural in origin.

23 Freedom in Society

Of what importance is freedom to a man? To answer this question, we begin by reviewing the pattern of human life, outlined in chapter 7 as follows: "By choosing to think, a man learns about himself and his environment, selecting values (and disvalues) accordingly. Understanding that the attaining of values (and the avoiding of disvalues) requires action, he proceeds to undertake such action as and when appropriate."

THOUGHT–VALUES–ACTION. These three words sum up the human mode of living. It is through thought that one selects values; values, in turn, motivate action; such action sustains and forwards one's life. Each phase is necessary, and the impairment of any one of them is a hindrance to life. Specifically, impairment of the action phase is, generally speaking, contrary to the requirements of human life. We thus draw the following conclusion:

To live the life proper to a man, one requires the highest feasible degree of freedom.

When the restraints on a man's actions are fewest and least, he is best able to gear his actions to the achievement of his values. The higher his degree of freedom, the better the opportunity for him to translate his thoughts and values into life-serving actions. The lower his degree of freedom, the more likelihood there is that his opportunities for life-serving action will fall short of what his particular value code demands. It has been said that a chain is no stronger than its weakest link. Thought, values, and action are the links of the chain that supports a human life. It hardly avails a man if the first two links are strong while the link of action is weakened by excessive restrictions, for then his entire life is crippled.

Human life requires the highest feasible degree of freedom.

But just what do we mean by "feasible"? Doesn't the foregoing discussion indicate that anything less than full freedom is unworthy of a man? As a matter of fact, it does not. In a social context full freedom is not feasible. Rather, a social context requires certain specific limitations on freedom, as we shall now see.

Alone on a desert island, a man would enjoy full freedom, and this would pose no problem because, in the absence of other people, he alone would bear the consequences, for good or ill, of his actions.

But in a social context things are different: one man's actions can affect another man. A man on a desert island can throw stones without affecting anybody else. But suppose that in a social context, someone decides to throw stones at *you* because he feels that he will gain in some way from such action. What then?

Clearly the problem is this: Presumably each member of a society wishes to advance his life. What if one man (or group of men) tries to live by means of harming another man?

The first step in arriving at a solution to this problem is to see that such an attempt cannot be rationally justified.

Consider two men. Both have the same nature. Both (we assume) want to live and prosper. Both face the fundamental alternatives of life and death. These facts establish a kind of metaphysical equality between any two men.

Now, suppose that A tries to live at the involuntary expense of B, and suppose it is claimed that such an attempt is justified. Such a claim must rest on the assumption that A and B are unequal in some fundamental way, some way that justifies A's throttling the life of B. Unless it can be shown that A is somehow superior to B, his attempt to live at B's involuntary expense simply cannot be justified.

But there is no basis on which to claim, let alone prove, such inequality; the metaphysical equality that exists among men precludes it. Hence the attempt of one man to live at the involuntary expense of another is irrational—and therefore immoral.

The moral principle is no different if the members of some group decide to gang up on an individual. Mere numerical superiority cannot justify such a thing. When any group acts, this means that the individual members of the group have each chosen to act in concert with the others. Now, as we have seen, no one person can rationally try to live at the expense of some victim. It does not matter whether he does so in concert with others or not. Neither alone nor in a group can he properly take such action because, alone or in a group, he is the same man. A man does not become a superman by having accomplices in his actions. What is wrong for him to do alone, is wrong for him to do with the complicity of others. Even as the member of a group, he is still the same man, and the cooperation of countless co-conspirators in his actions does not change that.

Since the above observations can be made about each and every member of a group, it follows that *no group can morally undertake any action which is morally impermissible to an individual acting alone.* A whole is no greater than the sum of its parts. If it is wrong for one man to live by harming another, then it is *that much worse* for ten men to do so. An evil perpetrated by many men is more evil, not less, because of the number of collaborators. Since no one man has claim to the life of another, it follows that neither do ten, nor a thousand, nor a million men. A million times nothing is still nothing, and nothing is what any man's claim to the life of a victim amounts to.

Now we glimpse a solution to the central problem of life in a society, the problem of risk to the individual of aggression by others. Since full freedom does not suffice to protect the individual from aggression, it follows that full freedom is not socially feasible. There must be restraints on aggressive actions, and these are the only social restraints we can justify.

Although a man should have the highest feasible degree of freedom, this degree of freedom does not include the ability to harm others with impunity.

What is needed in a social context are ground rules, based on reason and designed to restrain aggressive actions. One approach to the formulation of such ground rules is to compile a list of don'ts designed to keep men from harming one another. But such a negative approach is not optimal. For example, suppose we proclaim, Thou shalt not kill. What answer do we give to the question,

Why not? Certainly our answer would contain the idea that a man's efforts to live and prosper are rationally justified in some way, and that this justification makes murder impermissible. In other words, the prohibition against murder rests on and implies a logically prior idea: that the effort to live and prosper is justified.

This furnishes us with a valuable clue: rather than establishing ground rules in terms of negatives that imply logically antecedent positives, a better approach is to base the ground rules on the positives themselves. The procedure is as follows:

1. Identify some kind of individual action as being rationally justified.

2. Conclude therefore that interference with such action by others is not to be sanctioned.

The second point follows from the first by the Law of Non-Contradiction. Contradictions don't exist and cannot be the product of reason. Hence, if reason justifies some particular action on the part of an individual, then it must simultaneously condemn interference with such action by others.

The positives we seek are man's rights. A right is a moral principle formed by following the two-step procedure given above. As such, it names some specific kind of action, identifies that action as being morally justified, and consequently prohibits social restraints on that action. That is, a right implicity prohibits any attempt by other people to stand between an individual and his voluntary performance or non-performance of the action protected by the right.

The significance of this concept of rights is inestimable. This chapter, as well as the previous one, was but prefatory to the presentation of this idea. And upcoming chapters will be devoted to examining human rights more fully.

24   Rights: I

Rights are crucial. They are also widely misunderstood and abused nowadays. For these reasons it is essential that the concept of rights be clearly understood.[1]

The topic of rights is not without its difficult points, and the reader is urged to follow the reasoning particularly closely.

This concept can be analyzed as follows:

a) Every right refers to some action, as in "right of free speech."

b) That action is identified as being in accordance with reason. Another way of saying this is that reason *sanctions* the action—identifies it as being morally beyond dispute.

c) Reason cannot simultaneously sanction both an action and interference with that action by others. That would be a contradiction. If reason permits such interference, then the action itself cannot be rationally justified in the first place. But if, as in the case of a right, reason does sanction the action, then it must with logical necessity prohibit social restraints—physical compulsion, coercion, or interference by others—on that action. This is clearly an either-or situation; it can't be both ways.

d) Hence, by prohibiting social restraints on the specified action, the right sanctions a man's freedom of action in a social context.

Several observations follow from all this.

1. *The source of rights is man's nature.* If a man is to live, then he has to think and thereby select values, work to produce his material values, and be able to use or dispose of such values in the furtherance of his life. These facts are inherent in man's nature, and in order for him to live successfully in a society, his

---

[1] Much of the material in this chapter and the next was inspired by two articles by Ayn Rand: "Man's Rights" (4/63, 13 ff.) and "Collectivized 'Rights'" (6/63, 21 ff.).

freedom to perform these life-serving actions must be sanctioned.

2. *A man's rights impose on others the obligation of non-interference.* In the previous chapter we found that ground rules are needed in a society. Rights provide these ground rules in that each of a man' rights imposes an obligation on his neighbors to refrain from interfering with his performance of the action protected by the right.[2]

3. On the other hand, *a man's rights impose no obligation on others to assist him in exercising his rights.* Failure to grasp this point accounts for much of the present-day confusion about rights. The fact that a right sanctions a particular action does logically impose the obligation of non-interference on others, as we have seen. But it does not impose an obligation of assistance on anyone. A right says, "You are justified in performing such-and-such an action," but your being justified in doing something hardly obligates anyone else to help you do it. Only the negative obligation of non-interference can be logically inferred from the sanction provided by a right, not any positive obligation of assistance.

Here's one reason why this last point is so important. It is often claimed that rights can conflict, that one man's exercising of his rights will in some cases necessarily infringe upon the rights of someone else. This claim is wrong.

Rights never conflict.

If this statement seems hard to accept, remember this: Rights are arrived at by reason, and contradictions cannot be the product of reason. Contradictions don't exist. It is impossible in principle that reason could establish two rights which contradict each other. Only through faulty thinking can one arrive at an apparent contradiction. Hence, only by faulty thinking can one arrive at a conflict between two rights. The kind of faulty thinking that frequently leads to imaginary contradictions among rights involves the fallacy of assuming that one's rights impose positive obligations of assistance on others.

It boils down to this: Whenever it seems that rights are in conflict, it is simply because the rights involved are not clearly

---

[2] The manner of enforcing these obligations will be discussed in a later chapter.

understood in the first place. The proper definition and delineation of the rights themselves will show that they do not conflict. This means that when two people's rights seem to conflict, at least one of these people is claiming more under his right than the right actually provides for. Every case of "conflicting rights" arises because somebody demands too much, demands more than his rights actually entitle him to. He may, for instance, be demanding assistance from others in exercising his rights, when it is solely non-interference that others owe him.

We can summarize this principle as follows:

4. *Rights never conflict.* Apparent conflicts arise from faulty understanding of the rights involved, often manifesting itself by someone's demanding more than his rights actually provide for.

The belief that rights can conflict leads to another common fallacy: that rights are not absolute—meaning that an individual's rights can be "set aside" (i.e., violated) by others, if there are enough others to pull it off, and if they find it expedient to do so. The notion is that if two rights can conflict, then both cannot simultaneously prevail, so that at least one of them has to be set aside.

If rights actually could conflict, this would be true. But as we have seen, rights never conflict, though they often seem to as a result of misunderstanding. Since no real conflict of rights can ever arise, there is never any need to set aside any right of any man. In this sense, in the sense that rights need not and must not ever be violated, we can say that:

5. *Rights are absolute.* The only man who can set a man's rights aside is that man himself. He can do this consciously, or only implicitly through his actions—a point we'll come back to later.

The most fundamental of all rights is the right of life,[3] which sanctions a man's freedom to take all the actions necessary to forward his life.

---

[3] The choice of preposition used in naming rights seems to fluctuate between "of" and "to," as in "right of free speech" and "right to counsel." In the belief that the use of two prepositions contributes nothing of value to a discussion of rights, and may even create confusion, "of" is used consistently in this book.

Man is a being of volitional consciousness. He lives by thought, values, and action. From this it follows that there must be a moral sanction of his freedom to act on his own judgment, for his own goals, by his own choice. And this is precisely the freedom sanctioned by the right of life. Clearly, then, man's nature is the source of the right of life (1); this right is a necessary requirement of human life in a society (and the basis of all other rights).

The right of life imposes an obligation on each of us not to interfere with the life-serving actions of others (2). At the same time, it does not impose any obligation on anyone to assist anyone else (3). For example, I am obliged not to initiate the use of force against another man, thereby interfering with his life; on the other hand, I am under no obligation to offer him any assistance.

One man's right of life cannot conflict with another man's rights (4). If it seems to, it may be because one man is demanding assistance from the other. For example: Suppose I need a job, and I ask you to give me one; and suppose that you neither need nor desire my services and therefore decline to hire me. Now, suppose I claim that my right of life obligates you to give me a job (since I must work in order to live). You might respond by saying that by paying me an undeserved salary, you would be losing money which you could otherwise use to further your own life. You might add that *your* right of life entitles you to choose how you will use your resources (such as money) that serve your life. We now have an apparent conflict of rights, but the conflict has arisen from my demanding more than my right of life entitles me to. I am demanding something positive (that you give me a job), when all you actually owe me is non-interference. (For instance, if a third party offers me a job, you are obliged not to interfere forcibly.)

Let's consider another apparent conflict. Consider Jones and Smith. Suppose that Jones decides it would benefit him in some way to murder Smith, even though Smith intends no harm to him whatever. Now, we have said that a man's right of life entitles him to take *all* actions required to forward his life. Doesn't this mean that Jones is justified in murdering Smith in order to forward his own life? It does not.

By trying to murder Smith, Jones is asserting that Smith has no right of life. Clearly the only way Jones can justify Smith's murder is to deny that there is any principle that rules out such action—that is, to deny Smith's right of life. But Smith is Jones's metaphysical equal, and therefore Jones himself cannot have any rights that Smith lacks. Hence, when Jones denies by his actions Smith's right of life, he necessarily denies his own. He is denying the very principle he wishes to invoke as justification for trying to forward his own life: the right of life. This is the flaw in Jones's thinking. If he has a right of life, then so does Smith, in which case Jones cannot rationally make Smith his victim. If Smith has no such right, then neither does Jones, in which case Jones has no business trying to forward his own life in the first place, neither by murdering Smith nor in any other way.

What rights you have, your neighbor has too, by virtue of his being what you are: a man. The moment a man tries to throttle the life of another, he declares by his actions that his own life is up for grabs. A man who throws stones at others is proclaiming that he sees no objection to stone-throwing. He thereby declares himself a public target. That is why, in the above example, Smith *would* be justified in killing Jones in self-defense. Jones, by trying to murder another man, has denied the existence of the right of life. But the only person on whose behalf he can properly make such a denial is himself. By trying to murder Smith, he abdicates his own right of life and gives to Smith (or anyone choosing to defend Smith) the license to kill Jones himself.

When one man tries to violate the right of another, he implicitly abdicates his own right. On the other hand, there are many situations in which a man voluntarily chooses not to exercise certain of his rights. Such situations generally involve agreements among men. For instance: I attend a show at a theater where smoking is not allowed. In buying a ticket and entering the theater, I agree not to exercise my right to smoke. (And if I do smoke anyway, the manager would be justified in asking me to leave.)

This simple example illustrates the principle that, when one man voluntarily enters into an agreement with another, each agrees to accept the other's terms and conditions, and that these terms and conditions often involve agreement to refrain from exercising some particular rights. If one is not willing to accept the terms, then one does not enter into the agreement. (If I am unwilling to suspend smoking for the duration of the show, then I don't go to the show.)

Terms and conditions are either stated explicitly in advance, or else may be understood as matters of common practice. (It is understood that my buying a ticket entitles me to see the show. If the show has been canceled, then I am entitled to a refund.)

We can see that the topic of rights is not without its complexities and deserves much careful thought. Such thought has been in short supply over the years, which accounts for the incredible (and dangerous) confusion that surrounds the topic of rights today.

The purpose of rights is to protect the individual in a society. Where society is deemed to be above or outside moral law, that is, where rights are not recognized, brute force rules in one form or another, as witness the ugly facts of dictatorship. Rights make possible the orderly yet voluntary coexistence of individuals in a society.

25 Rights: II

In the previous chapter we arrived at some principles concerning rights:

1. Man's nature is the source of rights.
2. A man's rights impose the obligation of non-interference on others.
3. A man's rights impose no obligation on others to assist him in exercising his rights.
4. Rights never conflict.
5. Rights are absolute.

From time to time in our discussion of rights we'll be referring to these principles (by number).

Back in chapter 19 we touched upon the topics of production and trade. Quoting from that discussion:

"As a biological organism a man requires food—as well as clothing and shelter to protect him from the elements. These material goods have to be *produced*—made from raw materials by purposeful human effort.

"Living in isolation, a man would have to try to produce all these things for himself. But living in a society offers him a tremendous advantage: rather than having to try to produce all these things for himself, he has the opportunity in a society to specialize in his productive efforts so that he can then *trade* with others. In the simplest workable situation, trade would be by barter; the man who produced bread would produce more than he personally needed, and then trade the surplus to other men for their respective products, like shoes or fuel. A more efficient approach is to use a medium of exchange—money—to accomplish trade."

Notice what these facts imply:

— A man must be free to engage in productive activity.
— He must be free to use and dispose of what he has produced.
— He must be free to trade with other men.

To say that man needs to be free to perform these activities is to say that they are his to perform *by right,* namely by:
— Right of production.
— Right of ownership.
— Right of trade.

We're about to take a close look at these rights. Each of them refers to material values or goods, and for brevity we'll refer to such values (including money) as wealth. Notice that no special abundance of money or goods is implied by our use of the word wealth; rather, we shall use this term to refer to material values in any amount, large or small.

Since a man needs to produce wealth in order to live, the right of production is demanded by his nature (1). Although his neighbors are thereby obligated to refrain from interfering with his productive activity (2), nobody is obliged to help him produce anything (3).

But merely to produce wealth is not enough. Wealth is sought because of its life-serving potential. That potential disappears for the producer if he is not able to put the wealth to use in some way. It would be pointless for a man to produce anything unless he had the opportunity to use or trade it; a man's work rests on the premise that he will be able to use or dispose of what he produces so as to further the life of himself and his loved ones. He works to obtain food, for instance, in the expectation of eating it or giving it to his loved ones for them to eat. Else, what good is the food to him? Clearly, if material values produced are to be of any benefit to the producer, he must have the right to use and dispose of them as he sees fit. This is the right of ownership. Ownership is not merely possession; a thief possesses what he steals, but he doesn't own it. To own a thing is to be able by right to use or dispose of it in any way that does not violate the rights of others.[1]

---

[1] Rights can never conflict (4). My ownership of a gun does not entitle me to shoot you with it (except in self-defense).

A man needs this right by nature (1) so that he can use what he produces to further his life. This right obligates others not to steal what is his (2). However, it does not obligate anyone to provide him with any goods (3).

Rather than put all he owns to direct use, a man may decide that it would better serve his life to exchange something he owns for something owned by another man. The right of trade sanctions such action.

Suppose that I am a tailor and you are a farmer. My shop is full of clothes, but I need food in order to live. You have a surplus of food but may need a new coat. So we agree to trade: you will give me a quantity of food in exchange for a coat. This simple example illustrates several key points:

a) Both of us gain from the trade. It is sometimes argued by the economically ignorant that if one party to a trade gains, then the other must lose. After all, it is said, if the coat is of greater value than the food, then the tailor loses in the above trade by trading a greater value for a lesser one; but if the food is of greater value than the coat, then the farmer loses. Either way, it is claimed, someone loses. What this argument overlooks is that values are relative to the man who holds them. In the above example I have a surplus of clothing—more than I can directly use—but I need food. Hence the food is of greater value to *me* than is the coat. On the other hand, that same coat is of greater value to *you* than is the food because you need the coat but have a surplus of food. Hence, in making the trade, each of us gains because each of us is trading what is *to him* a lesser value for what is *to him* a greater value, and trading a lesser value for a greater one constitutes a gain, not a loss. Hence in a trade each trader considers the exchange to be to his advantage; the advantage in a trade is mutual, not one-sided.

b) To ensure that each of us does in fact consider the trade to be to his advantage, it is essential that we *agree* to make the trade. We must agree on which coat is to be traded, and on how much and what kinds of food are to be given for it. In the absence of such agreement, there will simply be no trade. For either of us to force the other to trade would constitute theft. Remember that a man's right of ownership entitles him to be the sole arbiter of how his wealth is to be disposed of (consonant with the rights of others). Taking any of his wealth from him without his consent is theft, whether or not the thief leaves something "in return." Traders trade by mutual consent. A forced trade is not a trade at all; it is a robbery.

We can sum all this up as follows: (1) A man's right of trade entitles him to trade with any other man who is willing to trade with him. All other persons must refrain from interfering with trade (2), but a man's right of trade does not obligate anyone to trade with him. A trade requires the consent of both traders.

There is a word for the condition of those who do not enjoy the rights discussed above. The word is "slavery," and slavery can exist in degrees. To the extent that a man is not allowed to own all that he produces, or is forced to enter any trade, to that extent he is a slave. To that extent he is involuntarily serving others (the ones who expropriate his wealth or force him to trade against his will), and involuntary servitude is the essence of slavery.

A few comments are in order on the nature of productive activity. We have described production of the simplest kind: making goods out of raw materials. Examples of such production include the growing of food, the weaving of cloth, the building of homes. However, we should not overlook such forms of production as mining, in which the materials are not made (they are already present in the ground) but rather are made available for human use. Likewise, shippers, who transport goods to where they're needed are certainly productive. Nor should we forget such activities as medicine and teaching, in which services, rather than merchandise, are offered to those who want them. In an advanced society, productive activity takes many, many forms. Farmers, doctors, miners, teachers, stenographers, scientists, machinists, artists, janitors, writers, actors, bootblacks—these are productive people. On the other hand, thieves and extortionists, who gain wealth by violating the rights of others, are not productive. What productive people have in common is this: they

Rights: II

work to earn material values (wealth) in order to forward the lives of themselves and their loved ones, and they do so without violating anyone's rights.

The rights of production, ownership, and trade, which we may term collectively as "property rights," are interrelated. Consider this example: We have said that a man has the right of production. One form of production is farming. But suppose that the land one man wishes to farm is owned by another man. Can a man morally farm the land owned by another? Yes, of course—with the owner's consent. The two men would have to agree on terms. One possible arrangement would be for the first man to be the employee of the second, working for wages—trading his labor for pay.

This example illustrates another facet of the right of trade: (1) Rather than trading goods or money, a man may trade his services, his labor, for pay. Indeed, this employer-employee relationship is very common. Of course, no one is justified in forcibly interfering with such a mutually agreed-upon arrangement (2). Further, no man can force another either to hire him or to work for him; as with all other forms of trade, the employer-employee relationship must be on the basis of mutual consent (3).

It would be impossible to discuss all the situations in which property rights enter. Nevertheless, all such situations can be analyzed and found to be free of the conflicts or contradictions which in the popular mind are considered part and parcel of economic life. It would be well for the reader to think about various instances involving property rights, and to apply to such situations the principles developed here; in this way he can come to see clearly the validity and usefulness of these principles.

It is sometimes argued that property rights conflict with "human rights." But as we have seen, rights cannot conflict. Moreover, the attempt to distinguish property rights from so-called human rights is absurd. In the first place all rights are human rights. Rights are sanctions of reason—a distinctively human faculty—and relate to human action. At best the phrase "human rights" is redundant. In fact, it is worse than redundant, for it implies the existence of some of non-human rights (in which category the enemies of property rights inevitably place such trivial matters as production, ownership, and trade). The notion of non-human rights is akin to the notion of non-round circles.

So let's set the issue straight: All rights are human rights. Therefore, one cannot distinguish property rights from human rights, because property rights are a kind of human right. Can one distinguish roses from flowers?

Property rights are human rights—and very basic ones at that. Where they are observed, men are free. If they are violated, the death of all rights cannot be far away.

26 The Role of Government

Each of your rights imposes a negative obligation on others: the obligation not to interfere forcibly with your voluntary performance or non-performance of the action protected by the right. If anyone does initiate such force against you, then your rights are violated.

The act of violating someone's rights is termed a crime, and anyone who does it is a criminal. In other words, a criminal is anyone who initiates the use of force against others.

Although there is a rational imperative to refrain from committing crimes, it can still happen that some people (usually a small minority in any society) will nevertheless choose to be criminals. This raises the question: What should be done about criminals?

It is plain enough that something must be done about them. If it were decided to take no action against criminals, then everyone who lived honorably would be at the mercy of a handful of thugs, who could rob, rape, and murder with impunity. Clearly this would not do. As noted in chapter 23, there must be social restraints on aggressive (criminal) acts. Irrational men, however small in number, cannot be left free to violate the rights of others with impunity.

How, then, are criminals to be dealt with? Through *retaliatory* force.

In a civilized society, in which rights are recognized, the initiation of force is barred from social relationships. The criminal is the person who nevertheless does initiate the use or threat of force. By doing so, he gives others the option of using force against him. As noted earlier, the man who throws stones at others is, with logical necessity, declaring himself a public target.[1]

---
[1] See the latter part of chap. 24.

Through the judicious use of retaliatory force the criminal can be restrained and would-be criminals discouraged.

But this raises still another question: How should retaliatory force be used, and by whom? One answer is that the victim, or anyone who chooses to intervene on his behalf, should be the one to strike back at the criminal. In some cases, this is no doubt justified. If someone is trying to assault you, you are certainly justified in defending yourself. In such a situation, there is a clear and immediate danger to you, and your right of self-defense clearly justifies your use of retaliatory force to ward off the danger.

But generally speaking, the use of retaliatory force cannot be left to the discretion of the individual. This is especially true after the crime has occurred and can therefore no longer be prevented by the use of force on the part of the victim. In such a situation, it is extremely unwise for a man to "judge his own case" and become an avenger. The reason for this is human fallibility. Suppose that someone kills your brother and that you think you know who did it. Suppose further that you kill the suspect in retaliation, only to discover subsequently that he was actually innocent. What then?

Clearly the use of retaliatory force requires objectivity above all. In the first place there must be objective rules of evidence. Hearsay or guesswork, for instance, should not be treated as fact.

Then there must be impartial and disinterested persons to judge the evidence and decide the guilt or innocence of a suspect.

Finally there must be a code of punishments appropriate for various crimes. A murderer should not simply be reprimanded, nor should a boy who steals a bicycle be executed. Again, only someone who is impartial should mete out the punishment.

Although the observance of the above precautions does not guarantee that perfect justice will prevail in dealing with criminals, the objective control of retaliatory force sharply reduces the risk of injustice.

How then is the use of retaliatory force to be placed under objective control? Through the institution of government.

Objectively defined laws enable a man to tell in advance

The Role of Government

whether or not a particular action on his part would be legal—as well as what penalties he may incur for committing the act if it is illegal. In short, objective law enables the citizen to find out in advance what his legal position will be in any given situation. Sad is the plight of a man who lives under a system in which he can tell whether or not some act is illegal only by waiting to see whether or not he's arrested after doing it.

To summarize:

— A society cannot function properly unless rights are recognized and respected, that is, unless the initation of physical force in social relationships is banned.

— In any society there exists the danger of criminal action: the violation of someone's rights, the initiation of force by one man against another.

— Such criminal action must be met by means of retaliatory force.

— The use of retaliatory force must be under objective control.

— Government is the means by which this objective control of retaliatory force can be achieved.

This last point prompts some observations about the nature of a good government.

In the first place the justification for the very existence of any government, the purpose for which government is created, is the protection of the rights of its citizens.

It follows that the government is not the ruler of its citizens, but is rather their agent, deriving its powers from their consent.

The proper functions of government are symbolized by the policeman, the judge, and the soldier. The first deals with criminals by apprehending suspects and collecting evidence. The second weighs the evidence and administers justice; he also serves as umpire in civil disputes (such as those relating to contracts). The third wards off foreign threats to the people of his nation; he is, if you will, a policeman who deals with international criminals on the battlefield as opposed to local criminals in the streets.

The policemen and the soldier are needed to exercise retaliatory force. But this poses still another problem, perhaps the gravest of all: What is to prevent the government from abusing the force of which it is custodian? What if the men in government turn the power they hold against those who entrusted them with it, violating the rights of those whose rights they are sworn to defend, turning from protectors to plunderers?

A grim prospect, but one that must not be ignored. Government exists to protect us from criminals. Who protects us from government?

America's founding fathers adopted what is probably the best solution to this problem: a written Constitution containing what were intended to be ironclad restrictions on the powers of government and on the ways in which those powers could be used.

Many will argue that our Constitution has been only partially successful, that some of its provisions to insure limited government have been circumvented, that official encroachments on the individual have developed, that our police and courts have occasionally oppressed the citizen, that our troops have sometimes been used dishonorably abroad.

Agreed.

Nevertheless, the concept of a written constitution to limit government power is still a good one, even if the implementation of the concept has been less than perfect.

It may seem that the final solution to the problem of governmental abuse lies in the careful and precise phrasing of constitutional and legal provisions. But the fact is that no legal provision, however well phrased, is immune to circumvention by government. To put it another way, any limitation on government that one man writes, another man can find a way around. For in the long run it is not laws but ideas that determine the fate of a society. If citizens accept ideas that tend to condone the expansion of government power, then they will permit the most rigorous safeguards to be circumvented. If, on the other hand, the public truly values its freedoms and understands the issues, then even loosely phrased safeguards will not be defeated by bureaucrats— at least not for long.

Therefore, the task confronting us now is to take a closer

look at the abuses of government—and at the fallacies whose acceptance by the public makes these abuses possible.

In upcoming chapters we'll be discussing the status of the adult vis-à-vis government.

Children will be assumed to be the responsibility of their parents or guardians, because children lack the knowledge and maturity to make various decisions.

27 Censorship

From time to time the press reports incidents such as these: A magazine publisher is brought into court because of the content of his publication; a theater is raided, the performers are arrested; some bureaucrat utters veiled threats about government action to be taken unless television programming improves. These events are all instances of actual or threatened censorship.

Censorship is the forcible preventing of the production or trading of communicative works.

By communicative works we mean things that are created for the principal purpose of conveying ideas or images to people. Examples include books, magazines, pamphlets, photographs, drawings, paintings, sculpture, speeches, theatrical productions, films, recordings, radio and television programs, and music.

Whatever the work involved, the operation of censorship is the same: force is brought to bear to prevent the producing or trading of the work. For instance, the force might be aimed at preventing the publishing of a book (production) or the sale of a book (trade). Furthermore, the threat of censorship can well discourage the very writing of the book in the first place.

Although it would be possible for a criminal to commit censorship, say by threatening a publisher with violence, more commonly government is the culprit, suppressing a work and persecuting those connected with it.

The most common objections to the censored works are that they are "obscene," that they appeal to a "prurient" interest, that they lack "redeeming social importance," or that they present a "clear and present danger" of one kind or another. Whatever the excuse, the actual nature of censorship boils down to this: Certain people manage to impose their moral standards on others. These people seek to keep various works from us "for our own good." In other words, they regard the rest of us as too stupid (ignorant, evil, imprudent, immature, or what have you) to select our own works and feel that they, the chosen ones, must do it for us. These self-styled protectors of public morals regard the public as corrupt and untrustworthy.

They judge others by themselves.

Often these oracles are able to use the law and machinery of government to enforce their whims. Then their attitudes pass beyond mere private neuroses and become government abuse.

There are several reasons why censorship is evil.

1. *Men have a right of communication.* This right includes the rights of free speech and press. It means that a man must be left free to communicate with anyone who wishes to receive his communication. The right of communication follows logically from the rights of production and trade. A man has the right to produce a communicative work, as by writing a speech or composing an opera. He further has the right to trade his work with anyone who wishes to accept it.

Specifically: If I choose to write a book, and you choose to buy and/or read it, then no one is entitled to interfere with us. The fact that some third party may find my book offensive does not entitle him to interfere with you and me. Of course, he is entitled to refuse to buy the book himself and to try to persuade others to do likewise. But he is not justified in trying to force his standards on anyone at the point of a gun. And it is a legalized crime when government, instead of protecting *us* from *him* as it should, instead takes his part against us by suppressing the book or persecuting those who wrote, published, sold or bought it.

2. *The idea of forcing someone to be moral is a contradiction in terms.* Those who seek to impose censorship sometimes believe that they can make men good by their action. Indeed, some people suppose that the purpose of government is to "make men good." But no one can be forced to be moral and anyone who tries to "make" (i.e., force) others to be moral is acting immorally himself.

This is certainly true of the censor who tries to make men

good by preventing them from receiving "objectionable" works. Such a censor would be well-advised to reform his own morals before worrying about other people's.

3. *There can be no such thing as a crime without a victim.* A crime is a violation of someone's rights; those whose rights are violated are victims of crime. It follows directly that, if there is no victim, then there is no crime.

It should be clear that the act of producing or trading a communicative work cannot in itself violate the rights of anyone. As long as those who create, publish, sell, and buy the work are doing so voluntarily, then there simply cannot be any question of their actions being crimes.

Even if someone buys a book only to find its contents offensive to him, his rights have not been violated. After all, nobody forced him to buy the book. Perhaps he has been disappointed in the book; but he has not been victimized.

Some advocates of censorship have gotten away with claiming that "obscene" works harm society so that the public is the victim. Such claims are clearly spurious. If there is an actual victim, then it is possible to identify him and to show, not that his sensibilities have been offended, but that his rights have been violated. In the absence of such an actual victim (or victims), there simply is no crime, and it is fraudulent to try to circumvent this fact by resorting to grand equivocations about victimizing society.

It is sometimes argued that communication can be harmful. Suppose that some lecturer delivers a speech urging men to riot and that some of his listeners do in fact riot, harming others and damaging property. Or suppose that an author writes a spicy novel one of whose readers commits rape after reading its more graphic passages. Aren't these instances in which communication is harmful and criminal?

No—not in view of man's power of volition.

In the first instance, it is not the rabble rouser who should be blamed for the riot; it is the rabble who rioted who are at fault. The speaker may have urged them to riot, but it is they who chose to riot. Unless a speaker forces his listeners at gunpoint to riot, he cannot be held responsible for their actions, and it is wrong to try to shift their guilt for their own actions onto him.

Similar comments apply to the rapist. He, and not the author of the book, committed the deed. The author didn't force the reader to rape anyone; the reader chose to do that himself.

The urge to impose one's moral standards on others and to silence those with whom one disagrees reflects the base desire to dominate others. That desire must not be given legal sanction if a society is to be rational and civilized.

28 Prohibitionism

A few decades ago alcoholic beverages were outlawed in the United States, and they are still illegal in some isolated places. The possession and use of various drugs and marijuana are illegal throughout the country, as well as in many places abroad. Such restrictions are instances of prohibitionism.

Prohibitionism is the forcible preventing of the production, trade, or ownership of certain materials intended for internal use.

Alcoholic beverages, marijuana, and drugs are the most common examples of goods that have been prohibited. Although many people seem to see no connection between the prohibition of the 1920's and the drug laws of today, it should be evident that the two sets of laws are variants of the same principle.

The objections against these prohibited items are not without merit.

Alcohol taken to excess dilutes reason, if not drowning it altogether. A person who is drunk has impaired his most vital faculties and often is not responsible for his actions. Behind the wheel of a car he can be a killer. Furthermore, prolonged use of alcohol, as by the emotionally immature, can lead to alcoholism.

Similar effects can follow from the injudicious use of marijuana. The habitual user's judgments are affected. For instance, people he regards as friends while he is indulging his habit may suddenly seem insufferable if he abstains. Moreover, marijuana dulls discontent, deadening the habitual user to those facets of his life that demand improvement and correction. We have noted that no emotion is bad in itself and that emotions are useful if faced and interpreted. Numbing emotions that reflect discontent is a self-disservice.

Prohibitionism

There is a proliferation of naive and untrue arguments against the use of marijuana, and this leads some people to reject all the arguments against it as groundless. But the facts cited in the previous paragraph do argue against any but the most temperate use of marijuana, and make total abstinence seem prudent.

Drugs present still other problems. Some, like heroin, are genuinely addictive. The body comes to need the drug, undergoing agonizing withdrawal effects if it is not used regularly. This is tragic for the simple reason that any unnecessary dependence reduces a man's freedom. Nature has decreed that a man needs oxygen, water, and food. These dependences are natural and therefore not to be lamented. But to add still another, unnecessary, dependence to one's life is pathetic self-brutality.

Another drug problem: many users turns to crime for money to support their habit.

Hallucinogenic drugs tamper with the functioning of the senses, an effect whose evils we have examined previously.

Weakened rationality, fouled-up emotions, confused senses, the possible turning to crime—these are among the effects that prohibitionists seek to eradicate. And at first sight they seem to have some justification for their laws.

Or do they?

1. *Prohibitionist laws violate rights.* The rights of production, ownership, and trade pertain to all goods whatever, and there is no logical basis for excluding any items from the protection of these rights. If one man chooses to produce an item and a second adult chooses to buy it, then no third party has any business interfering with them. It does not matter what the item is, whether a pair of shoes or a quantity of narcotic.

The temptation to exclude certain items from the protection of property rights is very great, but it must be resisted. For it is in this way that rights are gradually whittled away. There is no logical basis for excluding *any* merchandise from the protection of these rights, and to try to do so is to compromise all rights.

2. *The fact that something is wrong does not automatically mean it should be illegal.* Isn't it wrong for someone to become a

drunkard or a drug addict? Yes, it is wrong; but that doesn't mean it should be illegal.

The purpose of government, and consequently of its laws, is to protect rights, not to make men good. It is irrational, and therefore immoral, for a man to make himself an alcoholic or heroin addict, but as long as he does so by choice he is neither the perpetrator nor victim of any objectively definable crime.

A crime occurs when A violates the rights of B. What A chooses to do to himself, however, is his own affair. It he chooses to buy drugs, he is not being victimized; if he does not force drugs on anyone, he can hardly be called a criminal.

3. *Prohibitionist laws aggravate the effects of drug use by creating a black market.*

Crime among drug users is so widespread because the price of illegal drugs is high; and the price is high because the drugs are illegal. Heroin, for example, is simply a derivative of morphine and could be produced by reputable pharmaceutical firms at a price commensurate with its chemistry. But, because its production is illegal, heroin is imported and sold at tremendously inflated prices (and deflated purity and quality).

By the same token marijuana grows freely in many places, and marijuana cigarettes could be produced about as cheaply as ordinary cigarettes.

The facts about black markets are these: If enough people want a prohibited item badly enough, then it will be obtained and sold to them, at a price many times higher than the free-market price would be. No market should ever be made a black market.

When a heroin addict resorts to crime to support a habit that costs tens of dollars a day, the blame is his. But where does the blame lie for the high price of heroin? With the drug laws. By outlawing heroin, they have driven its price so high on the black market that no form of honest work which the addict might be willing to do will bring him enough money to buy the drug. Unable to support his habit through working, he turns to crime. The crimes he commits are on his own head, but how likely would he be to turn criminal at all if the price of the drug wasn't so high?

Present drug laws have created a situation which encourages crime. The legalization of drugs would certainly reduce the incidence of drug-motivated crime. As a bonus organized crime's monopoly on drug traffic would be broken.

The abuse of alcohol, marijuana, and drugs is wrong. But so is the abuse of government power, and prohibitionist laws represent such an abuse.

29 Conscription

In the pages of foreign history we find accounts of press gangs: detachments of government agents empowered to force man into military service, especially naval service. Although press gangs as such have gone out of style, the evil practice of forcing men into military service persists. In America the draft board is the modern version of the press gang.

The draft constitutes one of the most egregious of government abuses. A man's right of life provides that he may choose for himself the course of his own life (as far as he is able to implement his goals), provided he does not violate the rights of others. The draft blatantly violates human rights in that it forces a man to spend part of his life in military service whether he wishes to or not.

The draft is a form of slavery.

This is not an overstatement. Slavery consists in involuntary servitude, in being made to bear unchosen obligations (other than penalties imposed by a just court). And compulsory military service certainly fits this description.[1]

For a man to be a slave, it is not necessary that he be forced to live on his master's property, perform agricultural labor, or submit to being sold to another master; it is not necessary that the condition be lifelong, nor that the victim be Negro. Such factors, commonly associated with slavery, represent but one form of this evil, a form relevant to American history of more than a

---

[1] For an excellent account of how an irresponsible Supreme Court managed to evade this obvious fact half a century ago, see "The Constitution and the Draft" by Henry Mark Holzer and Phyllis Holzer in the *Objectivist* (10/67, 10-15; 11/67, 9-14).

Conscription

century ago. But our own century has seen the advent of other, often more subtle, forms, of which compulsory military service is one.

The draft is not without its defenders.

Some say that military service is good for a man. To this I reply, maybe it is, but in a free society each man decides for himself what is best for him.

Others argue that a man has an obligation to serve in the armed forces. I have already commented on the nature of unchosen obligations: they constitute slavery.

Some ask, Suppose that we had a volunteer army, and suppose that the government wanted to wage a war for which enlistment was insufficient; how would the government wage that war? The answer: It wouldn't.

With a volunteer army, the government would have to persuade a sufficient number of men to enlist month after month to fight in a war; failing to do this, it would have to call off its war effort. The government would have to prove its case for war to the young men depended upon to fight it; these men would be the ones to decide, quite democratically, whether or not to permit the government to wage its war. The recruiting centers would be polling places in a great plebiscite, and young men would cast their ballots either for or against the war effort by either enlisting or not enlisting. Those who wished to join would be free to do so; others would not be forced. And if there were not enough enlistments, the government would have to withdraw from its war in deference to the manifest wishes of its citizens—specifically those citizens expected to do the fighting.

It is very unlikely that in the absence of the draft the government would ever again be able to wage war against the wishes of the public it is supposed to serve.

But then there are those who flatly assert that without a draft there would be insufficient troops to defend our nation even against actual danger to us. "It is all well and good to talk about fighting in Indochina when there is no actual threat to the United States," they say, "but suppose we were facing an enemy who had the capability to conquer us and fully intended to do so.

In that event there wouldn't be enough volunteers to defend us adequately."

The premise of this objection is extremely doubtful. If there were a real danger to America, it seems certain that enough men would volunteer—provided the government made our position clear to us and publicized the need.

We could, then, simply dismiss the premise of the above objection as too improbable to consider. But instead, we choose to face it: What if there were a real danger of being conquered and there weren't enough volunteers to save our country? Our answer: Such an unlikely situation would mean that our country had failed to inspire sufficient loyalty in our people to motivate them to fight for it. It would mean that large numbers of our men just didn't think it was worth the effort or risk to save America. And that would mean that America deserved to go down in defeat.

Shocking? What other conclusion can be drawn if you grant the premise that in the face of an actual threat to our country, too few men would care to fight for it? We have stated that this premise is extremely doubtful. But if you choose to accept it all the same, then do not turn your face from its implication that America is already dead.

No government has claim to the lives of its citizens. Government exists to protect the rights of its citizens, not to abuse those rights by inflicting forced servitude of any kind, military or otherwise.

30 Taxation

In order for a government to be able to function, it must be financed in some way. The most common method of financing government is taxation: collecting compulsory contributions from citizens.

What is the attitude of the public toward taxation? In the first place most people accept taxes as inevitable. As a consequence the *principle* of taxation is hardly ever brought into question. There seems little point in even adverting to the question whether taxes *should* exist. To many, debating the propriety of taxation would be like debating the desirability of oceanic tides.

For this reason debates and discussions about taxes usually deal not with matters of principle but rather matters of practice: who should be taxed, how much they should be made to pay, and so forth.

There is a basic fallacy in this popular attitude toward taxation: unlike the tides, taxation has been brought about and maintained by man, and as such is not inevitable. It would be futile to debate the desirability of tides; they are a virtually immutable fact of nature. Taxes, on the other hand, have been devised by man, and they could therefore be undone by man.

So let us approach the subject of taxation without preconceptions. The first point to consider is the moral status of taxation.

We know that because of a man's right of ownership, it is morally wrong for any of his wealth to be taken from him without his consent. But this is precisely what taxation does: the citizen is forced to pay money over to his government. Only one conclusion can logically follow:

All taxation is theft.

However startling this conclusion may seem, it is utterly inescapable except by deliberate evasion of the facts. Government exists to protect rights, not to violate them. Taxation is morally unjustified because it constitutes a violation of a man's right of ownership.

Many will insist that there is a difference between theft by a criminal and taxation by a government. Indeed there is: taxation is morally worse because a government, unlike a criminal, is entrusted with protecting rights. The criminal has no such sacred trust.

But, it may be objected, taxation is necessary. How can something which is necessary be evil?

It can't. And therefore, since taxation is evil, it cannot be necessary. The necessity of taxation is an illusion, like its inevitability. There is no such thing as a necessary evil. The very phrase is a contradiction in terms. No evil can ever be necessary, and no necessity can ever be evil. It is essential to grasp this point. Once a thing is found to be evil, it must be repudiated. It cannot be clung to as a necessary evil. Moral law is not something you can cheat.

Our reasoning up to this point has been in two steps:

1. The recognition of the immorality of taxation.
2. The consequent repudiation of the practice of taxation.

Since government must be financed in some way, a third step is now indicated:

3. The search for acceptable alternatives to taxation.

At first sight the prospects of finding a morally acceptable substitute for taxation may seem nil. They seem so only because so little effort has ever been made to find substitutes. Down through the ages the myth of the necessity and inevitability of taxation has been uncritically accepted, and as a result creative minds have just not focused on the problem of how to eliminate taxation. Progress occurs when men think about a problem and work toward a solution. Where preconceived notions discourage such investigation, no progress is made. And that is why governments are financed today just as they were thousands of years ago: by taxation. The practices and procedures of taxation have

Taxation

undergone change, but not the essential approach of forcing citizens to hand money over to government.

It is vital that men renounce their defeatist surrender to the belief that taxation is necessary and inevitable; it is vital that they come to understand that the abolition of taxation is both right and possible; it is vital that the power of thought be brought at last to bear on the problem of eliminating taxes.

Can it seriously be argued that the human mind, which has put men on the moon, is not equal to the problem of eliminating taxes?

Ayn Rand has suggested one possible approach to this problem (2/64, 7-8). It has to do with contracts. Most contracts are enforceable in court. This is a service that only government can perform; no private organization can properly enforce a contract.

Now, suppose that in order for a contract to be enforceable in court, it had to be insured by the government—certified and accepted by the government as enforceable. It would be entirely proper for the government to charge a fee for this insurance. The fee could be proportionate to the amount of money involved in the contract. No one would be forced to insure a contract, but only contracts insured would be protected by the courts.

Such a system would be proper, while taxation is not. Rather than forcing citizens to contribute money for which they get no specific benefit, contract insurance would involve a government's charging a fee for services. Private insurance companies charge fees for the types of insurance they issue; it would hardly be wrong for a government to charge a fee for the type of insurance which it alone can offer.

But, it may be asked, how much money could be raised in this way?

The number of contracts that exist and the amount of money they involve are staggering. Employment agreements of various kinds, professional commissions, service agreements, bank accounts, loans, installment buying, credit cards, insurance policies, many kinds of investments, mortgages, leases, industrial and commercial transactions—these are some of things protected by contractual agreements. All depend implicitly on the protection of the courts. Why shouldn't this protection be paid for in advance by the parties to the contract?

Of course, some of the revenue raised in this way would go to pay for the handling of civil suits that arise in connection with contracts. But only a fraction of contracts are ever contested in court. Consequently it is quite likely that great deal of money would be left over for the financing of *proper* government functions.

Miss Rand stresses that this approach is only a suggestion, but it certainly seems a promising one. The point is that men must start thinking about taxation as an evil that can be eliminated. Once this breakthrough in thought is made, the future will be a lot brighter.

31 Evaluating Government Practices

In the last few chapters we have examined some specific government abuses: censorship, prohibitionism, conscription, taxation. To devote a whole chapter to each government abuse that exists would take thousands of pages. Instead, let us now summarize the approach you can use to form your own evaluation of government practices, and then briefly cite a few more examples.

The way to evaluate a government practice is simply to measure it against basic principles on the nature of rights and the purpose of government, principles derived in earlier chapters. Does a particular government practice square off well with these principles, or does it clash with them? This is the question to be asked. In answering it, you must scrupulously guard against unwarranted preconceptions that bias thinking. The answer you arrive at is your moral evaluation of the government practice in question.

This is the procedure we have been employing to evaluate government practices. A few more examples follow.

Eminent Domain. The practice of confiscating private property for public (government) use is another instance of governmental theft. As always, it does not matter whether anything is given in return or not. If the owner of the property does not agree to sell it, then its appropriation by government is an act of theft.

Gun Control. A man has the right of self-defense. It is wrong for his government to disarm him, thereby putting him at the mercy of criminals (who, of course, will arm themselves in spite of any law). Laws that make it difficult or impossible for a citizen to carry a weapon, concealed or otherwise, help only the criminals who prey on unarmed victims.

Gambling Laws. Laws that prohibit or restrict gambling represent attempts to force a particular moral code on the general public. As such these laws are improper. Further, the morality on which they are based is faulty.

There is nothing wrong with gambling as such. Like any other amusement it can be carried too far, by people who gamble away money they can't afford to lose. But though such excess is immoral, there is no reason why it should be illegal, so long as the gambler pursues his course voluntarily. And to prohibit, or restrict, all gambling on the assumption that every citizen is an imprudent fool who is going to gamble himself into the poorhouse is an insult to the public.

Nor is there any validity to the claim that it is wrong to win money at gambling. Although the gambler may not be particularly productive when engaged in gambling, the acquisition of money can hardly be called immoral unless it is by force or fraud.

Unwarranted Government Services. Many people seem to regard government as a service organization, with the result that governments today offer a conglomeration of services—old-age insurance, medical care, educational facilities, postal service, etcetera, etcetera. Not one of these services should properly be offered by a government. None involves the protection of rights. All can be offered by private firms, and many are. Even streets and roads could and should be privately owned.

To make matters worse, participation in some of these service plans is compulsory (e.g., Social Security).

The need for government arises solely from the need to protect rights. Hence any attempt by government to provide services not connected with right protection is logically groundless.

Further, since men can obtain services of the types named by means of trade, government provision of such services is unnecessary.

Whenever you hear someone insisting that government ought to provide such and such a service, raise this question: At whose expense?

Just don't expect a coherent answer.

Evaluating Government Practices

Welfare. Welfare services are an excrescence. They ought not exist, because they do not protect rights. Rather, government welfare is an attempt to materially implement rights by providing things that people have a right to work for but not to receive at the involuntary expense of others.

We have seen that unchosen obligations constitute slavery. Those who pay taxes for the support of others are to that extent slaves to the recipients of welfare. We have said that slavery can exist in many subtle forms and to various degrees. It is not an overstatement to describe as a kind and degree of slavery the status of taxpayers who involuntarily support welfare recipients. Think about it.

Commerce Regulation. Rent controls, which breed abandoned buildings; anti-trust laws, which penalize success for being success; pork-barrel laws that prohibit tradesmen from picking and choosing their customers from among those who apply—all are abuses of government power. All violate the rights of production, ownership, and trade.

A sale requires the consent of both buyer and seller.

No one, including government, can properly force a price on buyer or seller.

Success should not be deemed a crime.

Licensing. Similarly no one should have to obtain government permission before he can offer a product or service on the market. Production and trade are right-protected activities. One should not have to seek government permission in order to exercise any right.

Sex Laws. There actually exist in some places laws that presume to outlaw various sexual practices. Sexual practices that involve force, such as rape, should certainly be outlawed. But no sexual practice performed in privacy between consenting adults should be interfered with in any way whatever.

This applies to homosexual as well as to hetrosexual relationships. It is true that homosexuality is a symptom of psychological problems, but this has nothing to do with crime. Homosexuals who voluntarily engage in such practices are not harming others. Remember: there is no such thing as a crime without a victim.

And when all parties to an activity participate voluntarily, meaning that none of them has been forced, then no one has been victimized in any way. Hence: no victim, no crime.

Sex laws are an insult to reason and to man.

In evaluating various government practices, we find that certain popular fallacies tend to condone and perpetuate abuse by government:

That government can create or repeal rights. Rights exist antecedent to and apart from government. Hence, although lawmakers and leaders can abuse their powers by ignoring legitimate rights, they cannot actually repeal any rights. Rights exist on their own and not through official ukase. For the same reasons any right that government tries to create is counterfeit.

That the performance of some right-protected actions should require government permission. But a right-protected action already has the sanction of reason. No further permission is needed.

That it is right for government to initiate force against a citizen for a "good cause." This notion underlies governmental theft (taxation, eminent domain) and commerce regulation, as well as the draft.

Failure to recognize slavery. Any form of involuntary servitude is slavery (except for penalties and assessments imposed by a just court). Yet, taxes, the draft, and welfare schemes exist virtually unchallenged.

That government should make men "good." The idea of forced morality is, as we have seen, a contradiction in terms. The idea of protecting public morals by force is a symptom of the poison of Puritanism that afflicts many Americans—one of the uglier elements of our heritage.

That a right entitles one to material implementation by others. Once a person succumbs to this fallacy, he easily ends up condoning all sorts of government activities aimed at providing the implementation that rights supposedly entitle one to.

As an example, suppose I want to make a speech, and demand that a television network give me time on the air to do so, claiming that my right of free speech entitles me to use their facilities. Of course, my right entitles me to no such thing. But if enough

Evaluating Government Practices

people came to accept the absurdity that it did, then they might condone government's forcing the network to give me time—a clear abuse of the network owners' rights.

To clarify further this matter of what rights do not entitle us to, examine the following chart.

Right	Implementation—Not Included
Life	*Support* at the involuntary expense of others
Ownership and Trade	*Handouts* of wealth, property, jobs, food, clothing, housing, education, recreation, medical care, etc., etc.
Pursuit of Happiness	*Happiness* given to one on a platter.
Free Speech	*Facilities* (hall, TV studio) used without owners' consent
Counsel	*Furnishing* a lawyer at government expense

Government abuses are numerous and widespread. In a country like America they can exist only because too many citizens have accepted too many false ideas about the nature of man, of rights, and of government. The struggle for proper government is a struggle of ideas, and the outcome of that struggle will determine the fate of America, and therefore of the world.

32 Capitalism

Irrationality is so rampant today that one might be tempted to believe that a rational society is just not possible. But in the course of our discussions throughout this book it has been shown that reason is the very foundation of human life, meaning that rationality is not only possible but essential. The claim that no social system can be rational amounts to an assertion that only the irrational is possible—clearly an absurd contention.

What would a rational society be like? We can note some of its characteristics:

—All rights, including property rights, would be respected.

—Government would be limited, its sole function being to protect rights.

—There would be no slavery of any kind, no forced morality, no crimes without victims.

The system described here is capitalism. Before discussing the exact nature of capitalism, a few comments are in order about its philosophical status.

Ironically, the best social system ever devised, capitalism, is also the most savagely maligned. To make matters worse, the defenders of capitalism often use irrelevant or ignorant arguments in their attempts to champion it.

All this has come about because until recently, the true philosophical base of capitalism had not been stated and defended. To better appreciate the importance of a philosophical base, consider the following example.

Most people approve of scientific investigation; they believe that it is right for man to study nature and to use the knowledge thus gained to improved life on earth. In recent times, therefore, relatively few obstacles have been placed in the way of scientists, with the result that there has been much scientific progress in our culture.

Now, suppose that the notion had prevailed in our culture that

Capitalism

it is wrong to explore nature, that nature is to be perceived but not investigated, that man is not meant to know the secrets of nature. Scientists would then have been discouraged from their pursuit of truth, persecuted, jailed, or worse. And scientific progress would have all but ground to a halt.

The point is that no matter how good a thing is, without an adequate philosophical base it is likely to be betrayed and abandoned, either gradually or quickly, by the very public benefitting from it. If people fail to recognize a good thing for what it is, then it will slip through their fingers and be lost. Good institutions are secure only if they are understood by those whom they serve.

So it is with capitalism. Until recently capitalism had not been provided with a sound philosophical base and defense. Those who tried to defend it often did so in abysmal ignorance of its actual nature, and thereby did more harm than good. Then, too, there were, and still are, many philosophies inimical to capitalism, and these have hastened its decline.

That was the philosophical status of capitalism until recently. Then someone stepped forward to define, explain, and defend capitalism, not by apologizing for it but by proclaiming and demonstrating its splendid *rightness,* offering a source of fresh air in the polluted atmosphere of economic philosophy. It is regrettable that there weren't others like her a century ago.

Capitalism is *the* rational social system. Here is why.

A rational social system must be consonant with man's nature, not contrary to it. Man's nature requires that he have the maximum feasible degree of freedom. He will have this freedom only if his rights are recognized and protected. Now, consider the features that characterize capitalism:

—All rights, including property rights, are recognized.

—All human relationships are voluntary.

—The initiation of physical force by anyone, including government, is banned as a criminal act.

—Government exists for the sole purpose of protecting rights.

—All property—that is, all means of production, trade, and survival—is privately owned.

—Capitalism embodies justice by recognizing rights and thereby prohibiting government services aimed at robbing a man of what he has earned and giving the loot to those who have not earned it. Under capitalism a man gets what he deserves, one way or the other. And that is the essence of justice.

In spite of all this, anti-capitalistic ideas persist. At their roots are various fallacies, one of which we will look at now. It is what Miss Rand calls *moral cannibalism*. To arrive at an understanding of this phrase, we first consider the nature of cannibalism as we usually think of it: literal cannibalism.

Literal cannibals feed on the flesh of other human beings. The premise underlying this practice is that a mob is justified in turning someone into a sacrifical animal. The mob wants food; hence it is justified in murdering a human being for his flesh.

Civilized people recoil from the practice of literal cannibalism, at the slaughtering and eating of a human being. But unfortunately, too many people fail to reject the premise underlying this practice. The result is the perpetrating of other (more subtle) practices derived from the same premise.

The premise is that it is justifiable to sacrifice an unwilling individual for the sake of a group. The form of the sacrifice can vary widely and need not be anything so crude as killing and eating him. Nevertheless, the premise is the same: the premise of moral cannibalism.

This premise is generally stated in terms of "setting aside" some right of an individual or imposing some (unchosen) obligation on him for the sake of the common good ("public" or "general" is often substituted for "common," "welfare" or "interest" for "good.") But seeing through the circumlocution and the guff, we find the ugliness of moral cannibalism, shamelessly insisting that an individual has a moral obligation to surrender his rights for the good of the mob ("public," "majority," "nation," "community," etc.) and that the mob has some sort of collective right to make him do so. As if there could be a right to enslave!

The practical instances of moral cannibalism, the contemporary applications of its premise, are certainly less crude than killing and eating a man. Instead of taking a man's life literally, it may be part of his wealth that is grabbed (taxation, eminent domain) or a few years of his life (the draft). Of course, since the victim is not killed, it is possible to offer him some compensation: victims of eminent domain are paid some money, and a draftee receives a salary. But this does not alter the fact that these practices are blatant violations of human rights. To deprive an unwilling and innocent man of part of his wealth or of part of his youth is the evil of moral cannibalism, no matter how much compensation his oppressors offer in an effort to salve their uneasy consciences.

Evidently, moral cannibalism is profoundly anti-capitalistic, and so are its proponents. Capitalism is the enemy of moral cannibalism, and is no less an enemy when the evil is disguised by labels like altruism, collectivism, socialism, or what you will.

Implicit acceptance of the premise of moral cannibalism or altruism by alleged defenders of capitalism has led them to offer defenses that can well be described as grotesque: that capitalism offers the best allocation of national resources, that it promotes the common good, that it benefits consumers. (Producers are ignored; it seems that only consumers exist.)

Even if, upon defining the muddy phrases "common good" and "national resources," these arguments are shown to be true —the one about benefiting consumers *is* true—they are not the moral justification of capitalism. They may be among its consequences, but the moral basis of capitalism rests elsewhere: with the arguments presented earlier.

It is sad when a good thing is ignored, worse when it is attacked, and positively pathetic when it is defended for the wrong reasons. Moreover, this last can be the most damaging. A vacuum of silence can be filled by proclaiming the facts; attacks can be rebutted; but spurious defenses can confuse and mislead everyone to the point that the issues become tangled in a knot that can choke the goodness out of existence—just as capitalism may perish if not rescued.

Capitalism is essential to man's survival as man. It needs to be defended and restored to a nation crippling itself with a mixed economy. The enemies of the only rational social system ever devised must be answered and refuted.

33 Social Metaphysics and Spiritual Appeasement

Not all the problems arising from living in a society involve aggression and the violation of rights. There are also some psychological problems that specifically involve a man's relationship to other people. One of these problems is what Nathaniel Branden calls *social metaphysics*.[1]

The social metaphysician regards the opinions of others as being more important than the facts of reality. He is less concerned with what is true than what other people think is true (or say they think is true). To the social metaphysician, "they say" is more important than "it is."

One consequence of social metaphysics is that the victim's self-esteem is geared to approval from others. Since he regards the views of others as more important than the facts of reality, approval from others (or the lack of it) is his only barometer of his own competence and worthiness to live, that is, of his self-esteem. His self-esteem is grounded in the feedback he receives from the "significant others." If they approve, then he can feel that he is doing the right things. If they don't, then he is plagued by self-doubt. Such is the plight of a man for whom the opinions of others constitute the ultimate reality.

Hence the social metaphysician craves the approval of others,

---

[1] Branden touches upon this subject in many of his articles. Among those which are chiefly devoted to social metaphysics are: "Social Metaphysics" (11/62, 47 ff.); "Social Metaphysical Fear" (7/64, 27-28); "Rogues' Gallery" (2/65, 5-6; 3/65, 11-12); "The Roots of Social Metaphysics" (10/67, 1-6).

Social Metaphysics and Spiritual Appeasement

dreads its loss or decline, and in general suffers the anxiety that characterizes those who have alienated themselves from reality.

Social metaphysics does not develop in a person's mind abruptly. It starts in childhood and develops gradually. Frequently a child finds himself in situations in which he must choose between "they say" and "it is" (the "they" often being his elders). If he typically chooses to see things through his own eyes—and mind—then it is unlikely that social metaphysics will develop. If, however, he habitually surrenders his consciousness to the minds of others, then he may well develop into some kind of social metaphysician.

(It is granted, of course, that a child, lacking in knowledge and experience, will often make mistakes in his appraisals and must learn from his elders. What we are talking about here is not learning from others but rather giving in to them, surrendering one's mind to theirs.)

Why does someone turn to the intellectual renunciation that hardens into social metaphysics? Branden cites four reasons (10/67, 2):

1. Thinking requires mental effort—work; passively accepting the opinions of others does not.

2. A firm commitment to reason and thought does not permit irrational gratifications, such as the indulgence of whims.

3. The fact of fallibility, the possibility of making mistakes, may be overly reacted to, creating the illusion that it is safer to rely on the judgment of other (presumably less fallible) people.

4. Thinking for himself may lead a person to conclusions with which others disagree. In other words, intellectual independence may lead to disapproval from others and unpopularity.

Mental effort versus laziness; rationality versus irrational indulgences; confidence versus excessive fear of making errors; intellectual independence versus popularity and acceptance—these are sets of motives that men must choose among, and some men make better choices than others. Remember that the power of volition consists in being able to choose to think or not to think. How does a man become a social metaphysician? The same way that other men avoid this syndrome: by choice.

The most obvious type of social metaphysician is the conformist. But Branden has identified and catalogued other types, such as the power seeker (who tries to force the minds of others), the religious fanatic (to whom God is the significant other), the counterfeit individualist (who must discover what others approve of so that he can then decide to disapprove of these same things), and the ambivalent social metaphysician (who is social-metaphysical about some things but not about others).

We cannot in one short chapter completely cover the results of Branden's investigations into social metaphysics. So let us close our treatment of this topic by noting that this subject merits much consideration because social metaphysics is a terrifically widespread affliction, as widespread as it was (until recently) unrecognized.

There is one other problem that we will look at. It is a problem discussed by Ayn Rand in her article "Altruism as Appeasement" (1/66, 1-7), a problem confronting chiefly young adults—most especially collegians, to whom these next remarks are especially directed.

Exceptionally bright individuals—because they are exceptional—sometimes feel like outcasts. It is not merely the loneliness that comes from finding so few people who are your intellectual equals or superiors. It is the hurt that can result from being treated as an oddball because you are brilliant. The slouches and the mediocrities, consciously or unconsciously resentful of those with superior ability, bunch together in the brotherhood of wild parties and gentlemanly grades of C, and judge (correctly) that there is no place in that brotherhood for those marked by brilliance.

But as we have seen, there is a social aspect to man's nature. Nobody wants to be an outcast. So what can the bright student do?

A few, a very few, realize that "the bunch" is not for them and patiently wait to encounter those few whom they can choose as friends.

But far too many other bright young minds set out on the tragic course of courting the bunch. How? By putting their minds in the service of the mediocre and the undistinguished. They

Social Metaphysics and Spiritual Appeasement 151

adopt "liberal" attitudes: those that favor the common over the uncommon, the average over the great, the leaden over the gold.

They abandon symphonies for folk songs rendered by tone-deaf guitarists—and they eagerly proclaim that the latter are really "great."

They turn from competently made films to senseless, plotless, artless flicks—and they praise the latter for their artistry.

They try to forget the role of initiative and freedom in human progress and fall all over themselves to support welfare schemes —schemes that benefit most those who have the least to offer. And with a self-deception that becomes easy with practice, they boast of their contempt for capitalism—because that's the chic thing to do.

They assure everyone that they really prefer chummy but undistinguished professors to scholarly ones.

And yes, they join in the ridicule directed against other bright ones who have not chosen to walk with them down the road to stagnation.

In short, they sell out. They purchase acceptance, approval, popularity, with their intellectual integrity as the price. They choose popularity over excellence. They apologize for their gifts and proclaim, "Don't freeze me out. Accept me. I'm on your side. Why, I'll put my mind in your service, learn to ridicule what I honor, repudiate my ideals, stifle my vision, and become your mouthpiece—if you'll just accept me."

This they do because they want to "belong," but they never ask themselves, Why? They never ask themselves whether it is desirable to seek acceptance from the bunch. They do not choose to evaluate the standards of those whose acceptance they seek. Were they to do so, they would realize that those standards are lower than theirs in the first place. And that realization would melt away any hurt they initially feel over being left out because they would realize that it is better to be left out of that sort of thing. But instead, they choose to be part of it. And the price they pay is great.

By the time they graduate they have become undiscriminating, mediocrity-smitten, anti-capitalistic, social-metaphysical liberals, blind to all greatness—including that which could have been theirs —burdened by a sense of guilt, anxious to please, and fearful of ever being suspected of being anything other than the intellectual menservants of the "common good."

Could I be talking about someone you know?

34 A Rational Way of Life

The call of objectivism is a call to reason.

What do you commit yourself to when you choose objectivism? A life of reason, of purpose, of self-esteem. A life characterized by the best human qualities:

— *Rationality*. Full reliance on reason, the maintenance of sharp mental focus, an earnest respect for facts, and the repudiation of the irrational in all phases of your life.

— *Independence*. Reliance on your own mind: accepting no one else's consciousnses as a substitute for yours.

— *Integrity*. The refusal ever to allow your actions to contradict your convictions.

— *Honesty*. The refusal to betray reason and reality by trying to gain *any* value by means of deception or fraud.

— *Justice*. The willingness to judge each man for what he is and to treat him accordingly, refusing to grant or accept unearned respect, honor, or love.

— *Productiveness*. Recognition that material values must be earned by your own effort.

— *Pride*. A constant striving to perfect your mind and values because you know you're worth the effort.

These qualities, named and more fully discussed by Miss Rand in Galt's speech, are what a person chooses to cultivate and sustain when he chooses objectivism.

When you adopt objectivist principles, you adopt the metaphysics of objective reality, the epistemology of reason, and the ethics of *rational selfishness: rational* because reason is your absolute, beyond compromise or cheating; *selfishness* because you know that you are an end in yourself and you therefore work to achieve your happiness, refusing to play the part of a sacrificial animal on the altar of altruist-collectivist creeds that demand you put the happiness of others ahead of your own.

In choosing objectivism you choose to follow your conscience wherever it may lead—and to accept the consequences of doing so, whatever they may be, knowing that the spiritual consequences of betraying your conscience would in the long run be far worse.

In terms of a political system you commit yourself to capitalism—to freedom, rights, and justice.

Is this any way to live a life? *You bet it is!*